The Discovery: Beyond the Jesus of Flapjacks and Grilled Cheese

Joshua Via

Copyright © 2008 by Joshua Via

The Discovery: Beyond the Jesus of Flapjacks and Grilled Cheese
by Joshua Via

Printed in the United States of America

ISBN 978-1-60647-221-7

All rights reserved solely by the author. The author guarantees all contents are original and do not infringe upon the legal rights of any other person or work. No part of this book may be reproduced in any form without the permission of the author. The views expressed in this book are not necessarily those of the publisher.

Unless otherwise indicated, Bible quotations are taken from The Holman Christian Standard Bible®. Copyright © 2004 by Holman Bible Publishers.

www.xulonpress.com

For Tasha Joy, my joy and crown

Contents

❦

Introduction: Breakfast with Jesus ix
1. Buzz Lightyear Recognition Software (John 1) 17
2. The Pseudo-Starbucks Experience (John 2) 25
3. Novelty and Familiarity (John 3) 33
4. Hey, Check Out That Random, Shiny Object! (John 4) 41
5. Storm Tracking with Crippled Guys (John 5) 49
6. To Whom Shall We Go? (John 6) 57
7. Identity Crisis – Part 1 (John 7) 65
8. Identity Crisis – Part 2 (John 8) 73
9. The Problem of Evil as it Relates to Chick-fil-A
    Cows (John 9) 81
10. God Loves Dumb Animals (John 10) 91
11. A Boy and Three Bears: A Parable About Faith and
    Doubt (John 11) 99
12. Where Feet and Hair Collide (John 12) 107
13. Reinstate Slavery (John 13) 115
14. Directionally Challenged (John 14) 121
15. Obsessed with Foliage (John 15) 129
16. A Time is Coming (John 16) 137
17. That They All Might be Target Team Members (John 17) 145
18. The Look (John 18) 153
19. More Dot Connecting (John 19) 161
20. Do We Have Enough Canned Meat? (John 20) 169
21. The Danish Red Fox and the Farmer: A Parable About
    Sin and Restoration (John 21) 179
Conclusion: Coming Back for Seconds 191

INTRODUCTION

Breakfast with Jesus

A few years ago a string of news reports circulated the U.S.—news about a life-changing discovery—a history-making discovery—a discovery to beat all discoveries—a discovery so surreal, it was destined to redefine the very word *discovery*. Was it the Holy Grail? Or Bigfoot? Maybe The Loch Ness Monster? Atlantis? Elvis? E.T.? Nope. Even better. People began discovering *Jesus*. But not in a church. Not in a synagogue. Not in a religious meeting. And not in the Bible. Nope. None of these. People began discovering Jesus ... (drum roll) in their FOOD! That's right! The blurry, pixilated silhouette of Jesus' face began mysteriously appearing on morning flapjacks, on grilled cheese sandwiches, fish sticks and wherever else the Son of God chose to illuminate His holy, edible image.

As you can imagine, the image of Jesus' face appearing in the crust of these divine delectables caused quite a stir. Maybe you remember what happened. Perplexed at the face staring back, these individuals struggled with what to do with their holy hotcakes. Should they go ahead and eat Jesus? Would that be sac religious?

The Discovery: Beyond the Jesus of Flapjacks and Grilled Cheese

Should they put Him in a Ziploc bag and toss Him in the freezer? Wouldn't *that* be sac religious? Or should they simply sell Him on eBay and make a quick buck? Yep, you guessed it. The Jesus grilled cheese and the Jesus pancakes were super-hot items on eBay. A couple in Ohio opened the bidding for their Jesus pancake at $500.[1] A pancake in Florida with the Jesus/Virgin Mary combo went for $338.[2] A decade-old grilled cheese sold for $28,000 to a casino in Florida.[3] The frenzy was on. Madness ensued.

Soon copycat pancakes were all the craze. Jesus edibles flooded the Internet. People began selling anything that, with enough imagination, could pass for the image of Jesus (although most looked more like a really bad Boy Scout foil engraving of Jerry Garcia). Though many of the breakfast-loving eBay sellers held to their story of flapjack authenticity, word began leaking of the fakes. The gig was up. But the spirit of the entrepreneur could not be thwarted. The Jesus pancake skillet was the next marketable item to be introduced on the web. Complete with raised stainless-steel engravings, the Jesus pancake skillet burns the image of Jesus directly on the pancake for anyone desiring to have breakfast with Jesus.

I find a lot of things humorous about the Jesus pancake frenzy. There's the obvious one: How willing people are to throw seemingly endless amounts of cash at a breakfast item. Then there's the other obvious one: How willing people are to go on national television stating that Jesus appeared to them in their pancake griddle. If that were me and Jesus appeared to me in Bisquick batter, contacting CNN to have my smiling mug mocked by the entire civilized world would *not* be my first priority.

But what I find most hilarious is this: What little information the average person *does* have about Jesus, they get from stuff like this—they get from seeing His face on a pancake. Actually, it's not hilarious. It's heart breaking and devastating, because the only Jesus most people know is the Jesus of the evening news. The only Jesus most people know is the distorted Jesus explained away by a History Channel professor. The only Jesus most people know is the Jesus of the tabloid covers. The only Jesus most people know is the Jesus used in crude conversation. The only Jesus most people know is the shadowy, pixilated, Jerry Garcia-looking Jesus—the Jesus that was no more than a distant figure in history—the Jesus that has no bearing on 21st century life except to make a quick buck—the Jesus that makes absolutely no difference in real life.

It is out of this concern to discover the real Jesus that I am writing this. Not because I have some newly discovered information about Him. Not because He appeared to me over breakfast at IHOP. Not because I read an article about Him in the *National Inquirer*. And definitely not because I think I've got Him all figured out. No. I am writing this because, ironically and tragically, the *Bible* has been overlooked in man's discovery of Jesus. People all around the globe have failed to investigate for themselves the claims of Jesus—claims found in God's Word. Instead, people would rather believe hearsay. That's why this book investigates the Jesus of the Bible. And if given the chance, it's a discovery that could radically change the way you view everything. And I think the best place to start in this discovery of Jesus is the Gospel of John.

Why John?

The Gospel of John is the perfect place to start for several reasons. One, no matter where you're at in your Christian journey, whether you're just kicking the tires and trying to figure out what Christianity is all about, whether you're a brand new follower of Christ, or whether you're a seasoned believer and you want to grow more in your journey with the Living God of the universe, the Gospel of John is the perfect study option. If you're still wondering what you believe about Jesus, good news! John actually said that he wrote this book for you. He said in John 20:31,

> "But these are written so that you may believe Jesus is the Messiah, the Son of God, and by believing you may have life in His name."

There's a lot of hope in that verse. This book will help you answer the question of who Jesus is and how His life, death and resurrection impact you. If you're new to following Christ, the essential beliefs of the Christian faith spelled out so clearly in John will help you get a handle on where God wants to take you in your relationship with Him. If you've been a Christ-follower for quite some time and are already deep in your relationship with Him, a study through John will only solidify and strengthen that relationship.

Two, what John teaches us about the person of Christ is essential to everything we believe. John is both simple and profound. It is simple in its presentation and readability, yet profound as to its theological depth and depiction of Christ. Discovering the real Jesus is foundational to everything Scripture teaches about everything. The truth is, if you believe the wrong things about Jesus Christ, everything else you believe about the Bible, Christianity or God will be tainted and skewed—this is pancake theology. And that's what we're sick of. So John gives us an ideal place to start in understanding who Jesus really is.

How Should I Approach This Book?

I have a confession. I have a zealous love for cereal. Occasionally my wife, Tasha, comes home from the grocery store with the big kahuna—the 32-ounce bag of Rainbow Treasures—and I almost have a conniption as my heart leaps and overflows with joy at the sight. The thing about the 32-ouncer is that you have to set a realistic pace of consumption. If your goal is to eat the entire bag in one glorious sitting (a worthy goal, to be sure), you'll certainly make yourself sick, you'll make those around you sick, you'll probably come to secretly detest the sweet little treasures, and you'll most surely lose heart halfway through the process.

The concept of this book is very similar to how you should eat a 32-ounce bag of cereal. We're going to take one book of the Bible, John, and slowly consume it together. We'll move through it chapter by chapter, add some commentary, pull out some personal insights, toss in some life experiences, and then bring it down to where you and I live. Since John is divided up into 21 chapters, the best way to read this book, in my opinion, would be to commit to reading one chapter a day for 21 days. It is said that it takes 21 days to form a habit. One of the coolest things that could happen with this book is for it to be the catalyst that you need to jumpstart a routine time with God—that you would start to form the habit of Bible study and communion with the God who loves you and desires to have a relationship with you. That's the intent. But it can't happen without your willingness, obedience and openness to the Holy Spirit of God working in your heart.

Hungering and Consuming

As I write this, my son Ezekiel is 13-months-old. He's at that roly-poly stage where he consumes everything in sight, in reach and in circumferential proportion to his oral cavity. Actually, sand is his favorite food group. And for the record, the sandy bowel movement is never the friend of the baby wipe. Log that away if you need to. Zeke is a consumer. He needs food. Literally, he eats almost three times as much as our two-year-old daughter, Areyna. He's good like that. He's most assuredly all boy. He finds food anywhere. Three-week-old chicken nuggets in the crannies of the car seat. Petrified Rice Krispies permanently hardened into the linoleum. It doesn't matter. He's quickly discovered how to fend for himself when his appetite is involved.

Next to discovering the real Jesus, my other goal here is to begin to stir up inside of you a hunger for God's Word—that your craving and hunger for it would be ever-intensifying and you would begin to fend for yourself in the consumption of Scripture and Bible study. This is primarily a devotional book. But it's a devotional book that differs from most. You may find that it leaves a lot to be desired in many areas. It's not a theological treatise. Nor is it a running commentary. It's not comprehensive in that it won't cover every verse or issue addressed in the book of John. And there definitely won't be those awkward Sunday school questions at the end of each chapter that can be easily answered with "Jesus" and "God." In fact, you could easily read it as you would any other book. But then you wouldn't be doing yourself any favors now would you?

So that's where your job of fending for yourself comes in. As you read a chapter in John and a chapter in this book each day, you're going to be forced to move in one of two directions. One, you could move nowhere (which is essentially backwards) by doing nothing more than reading the chapter. Or, two, the better option, you could read it with the intention of allowing it to push you forward into a greater understanding and hunger for God's Word. You could begin to read Scripture in a way that changes you. As you read, you could begin to look for the application in your own life and allow the Holy Spirit to begin to change you and mold you into what the text says you should be—what God wants you to be.

One final word on your responsibility here and then we'll jump right into it. To get the most out of this study you need to interact with it. At the end of each chapter there are two sections. The first is called *Feeding Your Appetite*, a section with questions and activities for deeper study. Answer the questions as honestly as you know how. The second is called *Your Discovery*. Use this section for additional notes, thoughts, prayers and anything God is teaching you. You may even want to use your own journal or notebook. It's up to you. But I want to suggest a few practices that have helped me in my own Bible study that might help you as well.

1. **Set-Off Keywords:** Underline or highlight words that occur several times within a paragraph, chapter, or the whole book. Here are some of the main key words to be looking for: *word, sign, testify, witness, I AM, believe, water, bread,* and *remain.*
2. **Ask Probing Questions:** As you read John, you should be probing into the text by asking questions and actively seeking out the answers. Here are a few to get you started. *"What is the author's main point?" "How can I summarize this chapter in a few simple words?" "Who are the main people involved?" "Am I reading my own bias into the text or am I letting the text speak for itself?" "What do the keywords tell me about this passage or chapter?"*
3. **Make It Personal:** Apply what you're learning to your own life. Without personal application, all you've got is information. It's what you do with that information that makes the difference. Write down at least two action steps at the end of each chapter that you need to take. Make them specific. Don't say, "I need to help people more." That's too vague.

You won't do it. Instead say, "The Lord wants me to donate my entire life savings to Josh and Tasha Via Ministries!" That would be a more specific action step! ☺

4. **Pray:** Prayer should always be the fuel that drives your study of Scripture. In fact, prayer should fuel everything you do in the Christian life. Richard Greenham, a Puritan, said this about prayer and Bible study:

> To read and not to meditate is unfruitful; to meditate and not read is dangerous; to read and meditate without prayer is hurtful.[4]

That pretty much sums it up. So as you read and meditate on God's eternal Word, ask the Holy Spirit to open your eyes to understand what it is you're reading and studying. And He has promised to do it (John 16:13).

1

Buzz Lightyear Recognition Software
John 1

"How dare you open a Space Ranger's helmet on an uncharted planet? My eyeballs could have been sucked out of their sockets!"
- Buzz Lightyear

There are times in all of our lives when we look back on a particular event or circumstance and simply ask, "What on God's beautiful green earth was I thinking?" Just such an event happened to me a few years ago before Tasha and I had children of our own. Next door to us lived a neighbor kid named Nathan who incarnated the word *adorable*. Nathan and I had a cool relationship. He was three and I was twenty-three. He liked big trucks, Buzz Lightyear and playing in rain puddles and so did I.

On Nathan's third birthday, all 500 of his preschool friends were invited, including me. But I decided not to go. Instead, Buzz

Lightyear, the hero of *Toy Story* and archenemy of Emperor Zurg, came in my place. Yea, you read that right. My buddy, Mike, who worked for an entertainment company, happened to have a Buzz Lightyear costume that he let me borrow with little warning as to the effects this costume could have on the psyche of the individual who donned such garb. As I made my grand entrance at the party with lazer beams set to stun, I quickly realized the gravity of the situation. The costume was nothing more than skin-tight white and purple spandex that magnified and highlighted every curvature of the human anatomy with sniper-like precision. As cameras began flashing, I quickly explained to young Nathan that Buzz was exhausted from space travel and sitting down seemed the best option at that point.

There was something else going on, though, apart from the shock and awe I incited by my looking like a dolphin trainer from Venus. There was something going on in Nathan's head. The moment I started speaking to him his eyes became glued to mine. I could tell the wheels in his head were spinning out of control. He knew it was me. He recognized my voice. He recognized my face. But somewhere deep down in his three-year-old soul he wanted more than anything for me to be the *real* Buzz Lightyear. But his connection to reality refused to let him. From that day forward, whenever he saw me he would smirk, "You were Buzz Lightyear at my party!" Try as I may, I could never convince him otherwise. He recognized me. Somehow in all that get-up he recognized me.

The introductory verses of John's Gospel are the centerpiece of the Christian faith. They offer the hope of a God who came to dwell among men. But they also portray the grim and stoic reality of a world who did not recognize Him.

> "He was in the world, and the world was created through Him, yet the world *did not recognize Him*" (John 1:10).

When I read that I think, how could the world have been so blind? How could they not have recognized the Son of God, the Creator of the world, the One who spoke their very life into existence? And then my thoughts go to the religious leaders, the ones whose occupation it was to know inside and out the Law, the Writings and the Prophets. How were they able to stare the Messiah in the face and not recognize Him as the One the prophets predicted would come? All their lives they had studied the prophecies of the coming Messiah, but somehow they missed Him when He finally came. Whatever ability Nathan possessed to recognize me, they lacked. But I guess when I stop to be honest with myself, I have to wonder whether I would have been guilty of the same blindness had I been there.

I can think of a million examples in my own life when something has been staring me in the face and I have been blind to its presence. For example, recently I noticed that my wife was wearing a spankin' new necklace that delicately adorned her beautiful neck. I, being a loving, observant husband, commented on how good she looked and that I had indeed noticed that she was wearing a new necklace. As I sat there gloating in the glory of my observation, she promptly brought to my attention that she had obtained the necklace a week prior to my noticing and had worn it consistently around her neck every day in plain view since the day she bought it. It was a test. Not really, but it seemed like one to me. I failed it.

My wife is a very patient woman. She is sympathetic to my frequent spells of blindness and temporary insanity. She is a godly woman. She notices everything. I think if she had been there in the crowd among Jesus' followers, she would have recognized Him as the coming Messiah.

John wrote to people who were blind like me. He wrote to remove the scales of blindness that had covered so many longing eyes—eyes that expected the Messiah to come, but were altogether confused about who the Messiah really was and what He would accomplish when He came. So John connected the dots for them— to eliminate the pancake confusion. With all the lines in place, the Messianic picture emerges and we discover that Jesus fulfilled all 60 major Messianic prophecies and all 270 ramifications of those prophecies.[1]

What are the Chances?

Here's something that just baffles me. Christian apologist Josh McDowell examined the statistical findings of Professors Peter W. Stoner and H. Harold Hartzler. They asked the question, "What would be the probability of one person fulfilling even eight of the 60 prophecies?" Here's their conclusion:

> By using the modern science of probability in reference to eight prophecies, "we find that the chance any man might have lived down to the present time and fulfilled all eight prophecies is 1 in 10^{17}. That would be 1 in 100,000,000,000,000,000." In order to help us comprehend this staggering probability, Stoner illustrates it by supposing that "we take 10^{17} silver dollars and lay them on the face of Texas. They will cover all of the state two feet deep. Now mark one of these silver dollars and stir the whole mass thoroughly, all over the state. Blindfold a man and tell him that he can travel as far as he wishes, but he must pick up one silver dollar and say this is the right one. What chance would he have of getting the right one? Just the same chance that the prophets would have of writing these eight prophecies and having them all come true in any one man from their day to the present time."[2]

Unbelievable odds! No false Messiah could have orchestrated these odds. But Jesus fulfilled them all—without any preoccupation with having to get them all right—without the *Dummies Guide to Fulfilling Messianic Prophecy*—without a prophetic checklist in His pocket—without any real effort. He fulfilled them all. Because He *was* the Messiah, God's chosen One. And yet somehow the religious leaders missed it. People still miss it today. The next time you go to the mall or somewhere in public, ask ten random people what they think about Jesus and you'll get ten different answers, many of them bizarre. People are confused about Jesus. Here's a perfect example. Hang with me as I get a bit technical.

About every two weeks a set of Jehovah's Witnesses visits my house to discuss the Bible. The problem is, they only want to use their translation, the New World Translation, which has numerous problems that we won't get into here. Inevitably, the conversation always gets back to John 1:1:

"In the beginning was the Word, and the Word was with God, and the Word was God."

I take that verse at face value. They, however, apparently do not. They believe that Jesus was not God—that He was a *son* of God, but not God. And they use John 1:1 to try to prove it.

Now *really* hang with me. Supposing that they are using the rules of Greek grammar correctly, JWs (or "Jay Dubs" as I affectionately call them) argue that because there is no definite article in front of the word *God*, we must automatically insert the indefinite article *a* kind of like you would do with Spanish. If this were the case, John 1:1 would read,

"and the Word was *a* god."

This reduces Jesus to one god among many gods, but not *the* God. A quick glance at their text makes it seem as if they know what they're talking about. The problem is, in Greek, John's word order is in the *emphatic position,* which means nothing to you. It just means that he worded it that way on purpose. In the emphatic, you wouldn't add the article *a*. By using this word order, John shows that the Word (Jesus) is of the same divine essence and quality as God, meaning that He is God.[3] Bottom line? Jesus is God. John made it clear by *how* he said it. If John wanted to say that Jesus was simply one of many kinds of divine beings, there are more natural ways of wording it—a ton, actually. But he didn't, because John wasn't confused about Jesus.

Our culture has crazy ideas about Jesus. So we can't really blame the people of Jesus' day for not recognizing Him. Our own culture does no better, especially when we'd rather study the texture of our bearded hotcake than investigate for ourselves whether Jesus was the fulfillment of prophecy.

Now, what about you? Have you recognized Christ as the Messiah, the One who alone offers you the gift of eternal life and can give you purpose and direction?

Here's my challenge before you continue these twenty-one days. Ask yourself whether you have missed the obvious—that Jesus *is* the Christ, the Messiah. Maybe you believe it intellectually, but you have never committed your life to Jesus Christ and made Him your Lord and Savior. Maybe you've never handed Him the controls of your life. Examine your heart and then ask the Holy Spirit to reveal to you whether you have received Him or not—whether there has ever been a point in your life where you asked Jesus Christ to forgive you of your sins and make you His child. If you haven't made that decision, why not pause right now and talk to God and receive His forgiveness for your sins. Tell Him that you believe that He *is* the Messiah, that He lived a sinless life, that He died a brutal death by crucifixion and that He rose again so that you could have eternal life and know the joy of sins forgiven. Put your faith and trust in Him and ask Him to make you a child of God. And He will. He has promised to do that.

If you just made that decision, please e-mail me at josh@joshandtashavia.com so that I can party with you and with the angels in heaven because you were lost and now found (Luke 15:10, 32). I also want to provide you with some further resources to help you as you begin this journey in a relationship with Jesus Christ. Meanwhile, let's continue this journey through the Gospel of John together.

Feeding Your Appetite

In your opinion, is it harder for devoutly religious people to recognize Jesus as the Messiah or people who have no connection to religious things? What are some roadblocks for religious people? What are some roadblocks for non-religious people?

Read John 1:10 again and let the sadness of it grip you. What is the significance of John reminding us that "the world was created through Him"?

Be honest with yourself: Are there specific facts about Jesus that you are refusing to accept? Are there aspects about His fulfillment of the Old Testament that seem simply too hard to believe? Do you still have doubts? Hesitancies? If so, list them here and then openly ask the Holy Spirit to answer them for you as we move along in this study.

If you have some extra time, read Isaiah 50-53, and Psalm 22 keeping Jesus in mind as the fulfillment and focus of these passages.

Your Discovery

2

The Pseudo-Starbucks Experience
John 2

"I would say strongly, the success of Starbucks demonstrates the fact that we have built an emotional connection with our customers."
- Howard Schultz, owner of Starbucks

Right now I'm sitting in my home office listening to RadioJazz on iTunes. A group called TriFi is currently playing. I've never heard of them until now. Sometimes I like to cozy up in my office with a steaming cup of Starbucks Sumatra blend and turn on some jazz music, not because I have an exceptional love for jazz music, but because it's supposedly what one should do while one cozies up with steaming coffee in hand. Sometimes when I'm sitting here studying or working on music, I pretend that I'm actually sitting in a Starbucks or Caribou Coffee. I think I just work better when I convince my mind that this is currently the environment best suitable for the brain to function at peak performance. It works most of the time.

I confess that the Starbucks experience has rubbed off on me, as it has most of the culture. In fact, currently there are several best-selling books out about how to take the genius methods and principles of Starbucks and apply them to your own situation and context to create this unforgettable experience. I think I've done that unknowingly. Therefore my brain is now programmed to react only to stimuli related to or incited by the smell of coffee and the corresponding blues progression of a jazz ensemble accompanied by the incandescent glow of indirect lighting hovering overhead—the perfect mind-altering recipe.

Whether I want to admit it or not, what I've created is a pseudo-Starbucks. I can pretend all I want that I'm actually sitting in a coffee shop under the perfect conditions for educational advancement, but I would be merely lying to myself.

The same is true of belief in Jesus. Countless people profess belief in Jesus but instead have a sort of pseudo-belief. They have a pseudo-Jesus—a pancake Jesus cooked up in the kitchen of their own mind—a Jesus whom they have concocted in the laboratory of their own imagination—a Jesus who makes them feel better about who they are—a Jesus who promises to unload on them the bling-bling and the health and wealth—a Jesus who is a good entertainer and a good magician. The problem is, this is not the Jesus of the Bible.

In John's second chapter, we meet these kinds of people—people who believe in Jesus because it's convenient and because He does cute little magic tricks. These are pseudo-believers. But then we also meet a group of people who have a genuine, life-changing belief in Jesus.

Let's meet them. In John 2, Jesus performed His first public miracle—turning water into wine. At this point, most Bible teachers concede to the urge to rant and rave over the issue of why Jesus would turn water into wine, the potency of the alcohol and so on and so forth. I'm not going to do that. That's another topic for another time. And quite honestly, I don't see what the big deal is.

Ascending Greatness

As I mentioned in the introduction, the word *sign* is one of the key words for the book. John indicated a total of seven signs that Jesus performed. Some scholars want to argue for more, but there are at least seven. And with each sign or miracle that Jesus performed, there was an ascending level of greatness. Each one became greater than the next. Why? Because they lead somewhere. John had an end goal in mind for his readers, the death and resurrection of Christ—the resurrection being the greatest of all the signs showing Jesus' victory over death, hell and the grave.

One way to think of these signs is to imagine that you are watching a movie—a movie where the plot thickens as it goes along and with each climax or turn of the plot there's a greater element being added. Immediately I think of the great culture-shaping epic *Home Alone*. And of course its sequel with even greater national and worldwide acclaim. The third one was just dumb. There must be about ten of them out now, each with a budget totaling $500 while grossing a whopping $300. But *Home Alone 1* and *2* were life changing for me. I watched in glorious expectation as Kevin masterfully orchestrated prank after prank in this game of brains over brawn. The scale of greatness ascended with each flip of the switch and move of the lever. I think every kid, upon digesting the wonderful cinematic genius of *Home Alone*, went home to immediately begin working on their own contraptions and gizmos trying to figure out how to flood their own home without irreparable damage—or at least how to flood their bedroom without it leaking into the hallway. Or maybe that was just me.

Solidified Belief

That being said, John 2 presents us with the first sign. And following the sign, two groups of believing individuals are thrown onto the scene. Let's pick up in verse eleven:

> "Jesus performed this first sign in Cana of Galilee. He displayed His glory, and His disciples believed in Him."

The first thing that jumps out at me here is the fact that it's Jesus' own disciples who believe in Him. In chapter one they *become* His disciples. Now in chapter two they *believe* in Him. Was John confused? Did he report the events backwards? Not at all. In reality, their belief was solidified through this miracle. John was saying that, as a result of the miracle, Jesus' disciples were now fully convinced beyond any doubt that He was the Messiah—the anointed One. Sure, they believed in Him before, but now they realized that they would die for Him. There's a difference. Their belief was now solidified.

As a kid, I always believed that my dad loved me. My four siblings all believed that too. And I always believed that no matter what happened in my life, my dad would take care of us. He would be there for us. He would always have our backs. I never doubted it. He always showed it. To this day he's one of the most loving, thoughtful, heroic people you'll ever meet. He's genuine. So that summer afternoon at the lake when my baby brother slipped off the dock and sank like a rock to the bottom, I never doubted that my dad would save him. And before I had time to even process what had happened, my dad had already come to the rescue. I always believed in him before that day. But on that warm, August day, my faith and belief in him was solidified. That's where we find Jesus' disciples—with a solidified belief.

Circus Sideshow

The second group of individuals is the pseudo-believers. They are the ones who came for the show. They are the ones who heard about a great magician in town, a great miracle-worker, and they came out to see the circus—as if Jesus was some kind of freak show under the Big Top paid to entertain the crowds and keep the people guessing. Verse twenty-three picks up:

"While He was in Jerusalem at the Passover Festival, *many trusted (believed)* in His name when they saw the signs He was doing."

At first glance you might wonder how this is different from what had just happened a few verses earlier with Jesus' disciples. Good point. In fact, the same Greek word for *believe* is used to describe both groups of people. But in hindsight, John revealed the heart of Jesus.

> "Jesus, however, would not *entrust* (same word *believe*) Himself to them, since He knew them all and because He did not need anyone to testify about man; for He Himself knew what was in man" (John 2:24-25).

We discover through context and through this added bit of commentary that these guys had a superficial belief—pancake belief—a belief based solely upon the kicks and giggles that they got out of it—a belief as shallow as the motive that drew them to Him in the first place.

But Jesus wasn't fooled. He knew who His real followers were. He knew the motives of their heart before they breathed their first breath. So He didn't *entrust* Himself to them. *Entrust* is literally the same word for *believe*. In other words, because they didn't really believe in *Him*, Jesus didn't believe in *them*. John used a play-on-words that doesn't really show up in the English language. It almost has the same effect as Matthew 10:33 that says,

> "But whoever denies Me before men, I will also deny him before My Father in heaven."

To be blunt, if you have a pseudo-belief in Jesus, He will have a pseudo-belief in you. That's the bottom line.

I don't know which group you fall into. Maybe after two days into this study, you're realizing that you have a pseudo-belief in Christ. Maybe you're realizing that your relationship with Christ is dependent upon the miracles that He performs in your life (i.e. "God, if you would just get me in with that crowd, I'll follow you." Or, "God, if you don't restore my parents' relationship I'm going to turn my back on you, walk away, and never look back!"). That's pseudo-belief. That's belief based on what you can get out of it.

That's belief founded on your own ego. And Jesus doesn't entrust Himself to those kind of people.

Seems pretty gloomy, right? But the good news is, Jesus *does* entrust Himself to those who come to Him with the right motives—those who come to Him out of desperation sincerely asking this question, "Jesus, are You *really* the Messiah? Because I need to know! Not because of what I want out of it, but because I'm desperate to follow the true and Living God. I'm desperate to solidify my faith and belief in You, Jesus!"

That's the heart of a true disciple! And those are the kinds of disciples that Jesus is looking for.

Feeding Your Appetite

As you examine your heart and motives in following Christ, what specific motives has the Holy Spirit brought to your attention that have been misplaced, misdirected, or just simply wrong?

What action steps do you need to take toward maintaining pure motives as a Christ-follower?

Take a minute to read Matthew 10:32-33. How does this help to grasp what John said about Jesus not *entrusting* Himself to them?

Pray that the Holy Spirit will continue to solidify your belief in Jesus throughout this study.

Your Discovery

3

Novelty and Familiarity
John 3

"All objects lose by too familiar a view."
- John Dryden, 17th century British poet

The Texas Tavern—just saying the name gives me happy chills. The Texas Tavern is a small piece of heaven on earth. To many it is nothing more than a greasy diner that sits quietly tucked away in downtown Roanoke, Virginia, my boyhood town; yet, to me it is much more. The Tavern holds a unique place in history as well as in my heart. It opened in 1930 as one of the city's original landmarks and is still ticking to this day. As a kid, I loved it when my dad would take my brothers and me to the Tavern as a special treat. We'd each order a Cheesy Western and a bowl of chili—Tavern specialties. A Cheesy Western is essentially a hamburger topped with egg and relish—the incarnation of mouth-watering goodness in all its glory.

The Discovery: Beyond the Jesus of Flapjacks and Grilled Cheese

I can't count how many times I've found safe haven in The Tavern as I would sit and consume a Cheesy and a "bowl with" (Tavern terminology for a bowl of chili topped with shredded cheddar cheese, although I'm convinced the "with" is more an indication of the pandemonium that happens in the commode once the chili is consumed). Though it's over 70-years-old, The Tavern never seems to age—at least for me. It never gets old. Somehow it's like coming home. And no matter how many different short-order cooks they go through, the same great taste accompanies every scrumptious bite. I think it's imprinted into the DNA of the place.

Here's a poem that appears on the Texas Tavern website. It might help you to feel a little bit of the nostalgia that I feel every time delightful little images of this place dance in the corridors of my encephalon (brain).

"The Eternal Texas Tavern"

The Texas Tavern is a landmark forever,
It has endured through all kinds of weather.
The building color of red and white,
Will always hold your attention both day and night.
Friday, February 13, 1930 was a lucky day for everyone,
It's the day hamburgers and chili were served from sun to sun.
Through all its 70 years it has seen happiness and tears,
Sometimes at night there are signs of fears.
But the Texas Tavern has weathered the storm,
Even though it may look slightly worn.
If you have patience of mind,
We can seat 1,000, 10 at a time.
Gerald Williams has little to say,
Til' after his bowl of chili, he gets almost every day.
With Jim Bullington at the helm like a ship at sea,
He'll always be there to serve you and me.
Whether it's night or day,
The lost are welcome to stay.
The Tavern with its magnetic personality brings people from all walks of life,

> Once there you'll find it a delight.
> You can meet the rich and poor,
> Hungry people always asking for more.
> It has been called the Roanoke Millionaires' Club many times,
> For years its bowl of chili could be bought for dimes.
> Let us always remember the Texas Tavern.[1]

What a masterpiece (regardless of the superfluity of typos I had to fix)! I'm not sure who Gerald and Jim are, but the question is, did you feel it? You may not have. But don't feel bad. One visit and you'll be hooked. Now before you think about having me admitted into a psychiatric ward, think about the things in your own life that bring that sense of longing—that sense of wonder—that sense of fanaticism—that never-gets-old feeling. And ask yourself if you feel it when you read John 3:16. This is probably the most well known verse in the Bible, next to Genesis 1:1, and yet most of us give it no more than a courteous glance. I know I do. But recently God has been, how should I say, breathing new life into this verse for me—or more accurately, breathing new life into me through this verse.

I grew up in church. My dad was a pastor until I was fifteen, so I spent much of my childhood memorizing Scripture verses for Sunday school, AWANA, youth group, and numerous other programs. John 3:16 was one of those verses that was always just a part of me. I think my mom had me and my younger brother, Smooth[2], memorize it by the time we were about three-years-old.

When you're a kid, life is a novelty. Everything is alive with brilliant color. But novelties have a way of wearing off as we grow more sophisticated in our developmental process. Publilius Syrus, the 1st century Roman poet, said, "Familiarity breeds contempt."[3] I'm not sure that this applies in every situation, but he certainly had a good point.

John 3:16 should never wear off. It should never become so familiar that it loses meaning. It should never lose its novelty. Sometimes I think we allow ourselves to be unaffected by it, but it never changes. Thankfully, now as I read and study it, fresh insights pop out to me like the first time I heard it.

In What Way?

"For God loved the world *in this way*: He gave His One and Only Son, so that everyone who believes in Him will not perish but have eternal life" (John 3:16).

What hope! What a gift! What an amazing God!
You may be more familiar with this translation:

"For God *so* loved the world ..."

I personally like the former that says, "in this way." It's a better translation because it's meant to answer the question, "*In what way* did God show His love to me?" In this way: He gave His only Son. "*In what way* did God demonstrate His everlasting love for mankind, for you and me?" In this way: He gave. He gave His only Son. He gave His only Son so as to leave the glories of heaven, live for thirty-three years in third-world conditions with sin-infested humans and to endure the most torturous of deaths ever devised by man.

No other religion teaches us about a God who gave up His only Son to be killed for the redemption of human souls. It flies in the face of common-sense religion. That's what makes it so genuine, so real, so life changing, so believable. Pagan religions shudder at the thought of a God coming to earth to save humanity. In Homer's *Iliad*, a classic of Greek mythology, the concept of God as the Savior of humanity is completely foreign. Juno said to Vulcan:

Dear son, refrain: it is not well that thus a God should suffer for the sake of men.[4]

Apollo said to Neptune:

Thou would'st not deem me wise, should I contend with thee, O Neptune, for the sake of men, who flourish like the forest-leaves awhile, and feed upon the fruits of earth, and then decay and perish. Let us quit the field, and leave the combat to the warring hosts.[5]

I'm thankful that the true and Living God, the God of the Bible is not a God like that. He freely gave. He willingly gave.

The Confusion

Ironic is not even the right word. Earlier today as I was sitting at a coffee shop (an *actual* coffee shop) trying to figure out how I should begin this chapter, a very appropriate song came over the radio—Stevie Wonder's "Heaven is 10 Zillion Light Years Away." To tell you the truth I wasn't really familiar with it. For the three of you who are, e-mail me and I'll stick a lollypop in the mail to you right away. As I sat there, these lyrics jumped out at me:

> But if there is a God, we need Him now. "Where is your God?" That's what my friends ask me. And I say it's taken Him so long 'cause we've got so far to come ... I thought this world was made for every man. He loves us all, that's what my God tells me ... But in my heart I can feel it, yeah, feel His spirit wow oh woo ...[6]

I think Mr. Wonder knew he was on to something (especially with that clever "wow oh woo" lyric). I think he was close to the discovery without realizing it. I'm happy to report, that, yes, there is a God, and yes, we do need Him now, and yes, He does love us all. The problem is that most of humanity is confused about God's love. Yes, He loves us. He proved it by sending Jesus to the cross. But the confusion lies in the receiving of that love.

The main character in John 3, Nicodemus, dealt with that same confusion. There's no question that he was a brilliant scholar and a devoutly religious man. In fact, he very well could have been the most educated man in Jerusalem. He was formally trained in the Old Testament from boyhood, and yet he came to Jesus seeking answers. The man who knew the most about the Scriptures wanted Jesus to teach *him*. Why? Because he recognized a uniqueness about Jesus— a uniqueness that incited his curiosity enough to approach Him.

Having a truckload of biblical knowledge meant nothing to Jesus. He got straight to the point in verse three:

"I assure you: Unless someone is born again, he cannot see the kingdom of God."

Nicodemus' response is textbook:

"But how can anyone be born when he is old" (John 3:4)?

Nic had missed the point. He was confused. He was thinking entirely on a physical level. He was sitting there wondering how he could climb back into his mother's womb while Jesus was already moving the conversation toward the heart of the matter—God's great gift—a gift that cannot be earned or warranted—a gift totally of God's doing—a gift received by faith through, here's that word again, *believing* in Him.

That's the difference! It's not about our intellect. It's not about what we do. And it's not about how much we know *about* Jesus. We all receive His gift of eternal life the same way—by believing *in* Him—putting our faith *in* Him.

As you contemplate the greatest gift ever given to humanity, take a moment and thank God for sending Jesus, His One and Only Son. Don't let the meaning and importance of His Word be lost in the familiarity of it.

Feeding Your Appetite

Whether you were raised in church or not, what is your initial reaction when you hear or read John 3:16?

How does familiarity with Scripture both help and hinder our ability to see it in a fresh way and respond to it appropriately?

Explain the difference between an intellectual belief in someone and a belief that places faith and trust in someone.

Read over John 3:16-18 several times inserting your name in the blanks. Ask God to overwhelm you with the reality of what He did for you.

"For God loved _____ in this way: He gave His One and Only Son, so that _____ who believes in Him will not perish but have eternal life. For God did not send His Son into the world that He might judge _____, but that _____ might be saved through Him. _____ who believes in Him is not judged, but _____ who does not believe is already judged, because _____ has not believed in the name of the One and Only Son of God."

Your Discovery

4

Hey, Check Out That Random, Shiny Object!
John 4

"A paperclip can be a wondrous thing. More times than I can remember, one of these has gotten me out of a tight spot."
- MacGyver

I think most people, when realizing they've just entered an awkward or uncomfortable conversation, try to shift the conversation elsewhere. I think it's safe to say that it's a natural thing to do. For example, my wife and I are trying to potty-train our two-year-old daughter. I say *we*, but I confess I haven't been a big help in this endeavor. Sometimes, when we know that she's just pooped in her diaper due to the dreadful stench billowing from beneath her, we'll test her. We'll ask something like, "Rainy, did you just poop in your diaper?" She'll respond a couple of ways. First, she'll play the ignorant card, as if she speaks German, and stare curiously like we are babbling nonsense. Then when that doesn't work, she'll immediately change the subject as if her mother and I will suddenly be more concerned with planes in the sky, the tiny black speck in her milk, random shiny objects or the boo-boo on her big toe.

Diversion. Denial. Change of subject. We all do it when we're confronted with something that we don't want to face up to. We see a perfect picture of it in John 4. Jesus confronted a Samaritan woman with her sin—the ugly stuff that she tried so hard to hide—and she immediately diverted the conversation elsewhere. Here's some background.

Jesus and His disciples passed through Samaria on their way to Galilee—a big no-no in Jewish culture. The reason? Samaritans were half-breed Jews. Outcasts. That meant that Jews had zero contact with them. Even traveling through their territory was taboo. But Jesus didn't care. They were real people who needed a real Savior.

Passing through the city, Jesus stopped at a well to have a conversation with a *woman*—another cultural no-no. But again, Jesus didn't care. She was a hurting individual in need of the life-giving Savior—in need of her greatest discovery.

As the conversation moved from natural water to the Living Water, Jesus casually and most naturally confronted the woman with her sin—adultery. Sleeping around. Whatever you want to call it. She was in deep. She previously had five husbands and was now testing out a possible sixth. And Jesus knew all of this without her having to say a word about it. This is where she made the turn. Rather than allowing the conversation to remain on her and her lifestyle, the woman quickly changed the subject. She knew what was coming. She recognized Him as a prophet, and she knew that she would have to face up to her sin—sin that had left her hobbling through life, but sin that had become familiar—too familiar to let go of. This was all she knew. To let this man into her life would mean she would have some serious facing up to do.

Isn't this also how *we* typically respond to Christ? When He begins to pick and prod into our lives, we quickly realize the gravity of the situation. And often the gravity of it causes us to ignore the real issue—to change the subject—to point the finger somewhere else—at some*one* else. If we let Him continue, it can only mean certain vulnerability—certain confrontation—certain exposure.

The Samaritan woman was exposed. Here it was. All of her cards were placed face up on the table. Jesus knew it all.

"What do I do now? Quick! Change the subject! Distract Him from what He already knows," she must have thought.

And that's exactly what she tried to do—grasping at straws. She questioned Jesus about a popular religious quarrel, the big theological debate for that time period—*where was the appropriate place of worship?* She said,

> "Sir, I see that You are a prophet. Our fathers worshiped on this mountain, yet you Jews say that *the place to worship* is in Jerusalem" (John 4:19-20).

I can almost see Jesus biting His tongue and refusing a sarcastic comment about His being a prophet.

"Oh, really? You think so? That's what my mom keeps telling me too! Cool! Thanks!"

But He didn't miss a beat. She tried to redirect the conversation into the realm of tedious debate. She sent out a decoy. Jesus didn't follow it. He redirected her to the main issue. While she focused on the place of worship, Jesus redirected that focus to the spirit and the heart of worship. And when He did, the walls surrounding the woman's heart broke down and she accepted Jesus as the true Messiah.

Redirecting the Ship

Recently my dad and I were in Satu Mare, Romania on a two-week mission trip. On this particular trip, we were nearing the end and I was starting to check out mentally. I was ready to get home to Tasha and the kids like Paris Hilton is ready to shop. But God had one final divine appointment for us. As we were walking back to our hotel room, we met a man on the street that spoke enough English to carry on a conversation. We handed him a gospel tract and began to share Christ with him. Confronted with his sin, he immediately tried to derail the conversation toward theological quandaries about the problem of evil (which, by the way, I address briefly in chapter 9). Though I think he was sincere with his questions, he possessed a definite intent on changing the subject. After several long minutes, we finally redirected the conversation back to the main issue and he opened his heart to Christ and received Him right there on the street corner.

Though Dad and I had some difficulty in steering the ship back in the main direction, Jesus had no problem doing exactly that with the Samaritan woman. His reply in verses 21-24 "is one of the strongest worship statements in the New Testament" and contains ten out of thirteen of John's uses of the Greek word for *worship*.[1] That means this is a really pivotal and important passage. He said in verse twenty-four,

> "God is spirit, and those who worship Him must worship in spirit and in truth."

What was Jesus really saying here? Was He addressing her need to fix all the physical issues she had? No. Did He want her to come to Jerusalem and worship in the *true* place of worship? No. He was saying that God wanted her heart. It's about the inward, not the outward. It's about what God thinks, not what man thinks. It's about what God *actually* desires, not what man *thinks* that God desires. He desires worship in spirit and in truth—in spirit because it's the attitude of the heart that matters—in truth because true worship is always measured against the standard of Scripture and the person of Christ.[2]

Confrontation and Discomfort

Coming to God the way *He* desires involves confrontation, and confrontation involves discomfort. When I sanded the rough edges of my deck a few weeks ago, the lumber was, no doubt, cursing my name with every stroke of my hand. But now that it's beautifully sanded and stained, it bestows upon me praises and blessings every time I walk outside. Sanding hurts. It rubs raw. But beauty follows.

If we're blind to the beauty that follows, we may be tempted, like the Samaritan woman, to dodge the real issue—to avoid the confrontation. Or to take the least painful option—the more economical route—the cheapest route.

Recently, I blew a tire on my 1994 Honda Accord. I crept it into my mechanic's shop utilizing the hockey puck disguised as a spare tire so nicely provided by my Japanese friends at Honda. A few hours later, my mechanic called with some "bad news"—never what you want to hear from your mechanic. He told me that during the repair he had discovered a multitude of problems. To be honest, I wasn't surprised, but at the moment I didn't care what the problems were. I just wanted the bottom line. How much will it cost? He read me the figure. I stared blankly, gazing at my chest and wondering when my heart might kindly decide to start pumping again. I immediately asked what my other options were. What could we do to just get by? What corners could we cut just to make it through? What could we rig up? What would MacGyver do?

Herein lies our condition. We don't want God prodding around inside us because of what we know He'll find. We don't want the Holy Spirit doing the work that He does best because we'll be exposed. We want the quick fix.

To say that the Samaritan woman wasn't keen on Jesus prodding into her personal life is an understatement. She was exposed and she didn't like it. She wanted the quick fix—the most economical choice—the MacGyverism. But that's not what she needed. She needed a complete makeover. She needed the healing power of the Messiah to heal, mend and forgive—to remove the rubbish of her past—to sand the rough edges. She had made her bed and she was definitely sleeping in it. But Jesus was ready to pull her out of it. He saw the emptiness in her eyes—eyes that He was forbidden to look into by cultural standards. But eyes that screamed out for healing and forgiveness.

Jesus saw the emptiness in her heart—emptiness that she tried to fill with men, with relationships—relationships that never satisfied. He wanted her heart. He wanted her heart so that He could mend it—so that He could satisfy her with the Living Water—so that He could show her what true worship is all about—that it's very simply acknowledging God's worth in light of our worthlessness—God's perfection in light of our imperfection.

That's the kind of worship that God desires. Seeing Christ for who He really is always redirects our focus to what really matters—Christ and Christ alone. And somehow when genuine worship happens, His love transforms our filth to beauty and our rags to riches.

Feeding Your Appetite

Have there been times in your life when you've resisted the healing, forgiving hand of God? How did that work out for you?

What quick fixes have you been guilty of wanting rather than the full makeover that the Holy Spirit wants to work in your life?

How is forgiveness connected to worship?

Trying to avoid the prodding hand of the Holy Spirit in your life is an obvious indication of unconfessed sin. Ask God to reveal to you any unconfessed sin and ask for His forgiveness. Pinpoint the specific times during the day that you are most susceptible to temptation (i.e. late at night on the internet) and determine from this point on not to put yourself in those situations.

Your Discovery

5

Storm Tracking with Crippled Guys
John 5

"Legalism is to seek to achieve forgiveness from God and acceptance by God through my obedience to God."
- Keri Harvey

Legalism—the over-emphasis upon rules—the tendency to lean toward the shoulds and should nots—the checklist of dos and don'ts to ensure that you're in right standing with God. All of these definitions sum up the mental framework in which the religious leaders of Jesus' day functioned. Legalism kept the masses of religious people from following Jesus. And not much has changed today.

Legalism exists in every religion in the world. Every religion tries to find peace with God or gods through the keeping of laws and regulations. That's what distinguishes every religion in the world from the message of the Gospel.

Religion describes humankind's search for God; the Gospel describes the way God reached down to humanity.[1]

But the majority of the religious leaders of Jesus' day didn't catch on. John 5 deals with Jesus' first confrontation with legalistic religious leaders. All four gospels are full of these types of accounts. It happened so frequently that even if you've never read John or the other gospels, you could almost predict with a high degree of certainty when these jokers would be upset, because they were rarely *not* upset.

My wife is a weather fanatic. She loves anything to do with weather. The Weather Channel. Meteorologists. Thunder storms. Scrolling inclement weather warnings on the bottom of the TV screen. Wind. Sun. Rain. Words that start with *W*. It doesn't really matter how it relates to weather. If it does, she loves it. This is how much of a fanatic she is. During the labor and delivery of both of our babies she watched The Weather Channel the entire time—no exaggeration. And just the other day she signed up on totallyfreecrap.com to receive a signed autograph picture from a random weather person she's never seen before. She studies weather. She tracks storms. The whole nine. Recently, just to prove to her that anyone can be a weather tracker, I put together my own little syllogistic formula for identifying inclement weather conditions. It goes like this:

 A. *"Look, there are dark thunderclouds moving quickly overhead!"*
 B. *"Hmm ... a blasted raindrop just pummeled my eyeball!"*
 C. *"Therefore, I conclude that a storm is impending!"*

Simple. There's nothing to it. Cake. The signs are pretty obvious to me when a storm is brewing.

Whenever Jesus mixed with the religious leaders, an immense storm would usually brew and it was usually predictable. In fact, Jesus' conflict with the religious leaders can also be put nicely into a syllogism. It goes something like this:

The Discovery: Beyond the Jesus of Flapjacks and Grilled Cheese

A. *"Look, Jesus is performing a miracle!"*
B. *"Hmm ... it seems to be the Sabbath day—as usual!"*
C. *"Therefore, I conclude that a religious, legalistic storm is impending!"*

Like clockwork, whenever Jesus performed a miracle on the Sabbath, the dark sky of legalistic religion opened its ugly mouth and rained down putrid acid rain on the whole event. Why? Because work was not allowed on the Sabbath. Because they were more concerned with keeping the tiniest detail of the Law than they were the fact that lame legs, withered hands and diseased bodies were all made new.

John 5 opens up with the third sign in the book—the healing of a paralyzed man. For 38 years the man laid there at the pool of Bethesda hoping that the supposed healing powers of the waters would work on his behalf. But he had no one to pick him up and put him in the pool. No one cared about him. He was an outcast of society. A burden. Dead weight. Just the kind of person for which Jesus came.

> "'Get up,' Jesus told him, 'pick up your bedroll and walk'" (5:8)!

I love that. Jesus healed him right there on the spot. In the midst of his misery, in the midst of his self-pity, in the midst of his doubt, Jesus miraculously healed him. And a tremendous party broke out at the Jewish festival because a man who was once paralyzed was now walking fully restored! Umm ... actually, no. No party. Only criticism. Notice verses nine and ten:

> "Now that day was the Sabbath, so the Jews said to the man who had been healed, 'This is the Sabbath! It's *illegal* for you to pick up your bedroll.'"

> *ILLEGAL!? Are you stupid!? Do you not understand that this man was paralyzed and has been healed!?*

Completely restored!? Perfect!? With spanking new lower appendages!?

But the religious leaders didn't get it. They missed what was going on in front of them. The Messiah was directly in front of their noses but their noses were too busy sniffing for the chapter and verse of the exact violation of the Law. The man was crippled *physically*. The religious leaders were crippled *spiritually*. They were carefully tending to their precious pancakes while the real Jesus stared them in the face.

Now, here's where I want to draw some principles for us so that we don't think we are too far-removed from having this same legalistic attitude.

1. Criticism happened immediately following a great miracle.

Jesus healed the man only moments before the religious leaders went ballistic. And rather than joining in the celebration, the Jews dumped acid rain on the whole deal.

Maybe this has happened to you. Maybe there have been times in your life when you've been on the receiving end of Jesus' miracles, and it's been incredible—a mountaintop experience. Unfortunately, when you decided to tell people, not everyone felt the same sentiment. But everyone else's reaction *cannot* and *must not* determine yours. Rejoice that Christ has visited you and performed a miracle in your life. Rejoice that Christ has saved you. Rejoice that Jesus picked you up, as crippled and lame as you were, and restored you. Expect criticism to come, but no matter what the critics throw at you, rejoice that Christ found you in the situation you were in.

On the other hand, we have to be so careful not to be the ones dumping the acid rain. Maybe it's a result of jealousy on our part. Maybe self-doubt. Frustration. Whatever it is, we must guard against a legalistic attitude and rejoice with our brothers and sisters when God works mightily in their lives.

2. Rules must never take precedence over people.

Remember the impossible rules from preschool? Who could keep them? Don't push in line. Don't eat your friends' snacks. Don't poop or pee in the Lego box. Don't eat the glue. Don't eat the pinecone bird feeder. Etcetera. Impossible! My preschool teachers were pretty cool, but I think every kid wonders at some point whether their teacher cares more about the rules than the kids. But I can promise you one thing, you never had a teacher who cared more about rules than the religious leaders of Jesus' day.

These guys loved their rules—so much so that love for people took a backseat. By trying to please God with their tidy little checklist of rights and wrongs, they became guilty of loving rules over people—people made in God's own image. God had some pretty harsh things to say about this type of attitude in Isaiah. He said,

> "I have *had enough* of your burnt offerings and rams ... I *despise* your incense, New Moons and Sabbaths ... I *can't stand* iniquity with a festival" (Isaiah 1:11-13).

Ironically, the festivals and offerings that God came to despise were the same ones He instituted in the first place. He created them. He designed them. He set them up for the purpose of worship. But to God's people, their offerings became more than a means to an end. They became *ends in themselves.* Interestingly, when Jesus healed the lame man it was during the time of a Jewish festival. No doubt verses like these in Isaiah came to Jesus' mind as the religious leaders fell guilty of the very same sin—placing their commitment to the Law over their love for human beings. But that's the thing isn't it? They actually *weren't* committed to the Law. They were committed to an *ideal*, and the Law helped them meet that ideal. The ideal was this:

"If I do enough good things, if I keep every command in the Torah (the Law), and if I commit myself fully to it, God will be pleased with me (Earning embroidered patches to sew on my robe is a plus, too). And it doesn't matter how many people I have to walk on to get there!"

They were committed to this ideal, but not to God. They missed the point.

3. Legalism fogs Jesus' identity.

Because the Jews were looking through the lens of legalism, they missed Jesus for who He really is—the Savior, the Messiah. He had performed a miracle right in front of their faces and they missed it.

I'm not a multi-tasker. When I'm talking on my cell phone, I'm either hearing what the person on the other end is saying or I'm hearing what's going on around me. I can't hear both. So if you're ever talking to me and there are long pauses of awkward silence or responses that make absolutely no sense, it means that I'm probably not listening to you. Sorry. But I'm convinced that women have multiple hearing apparatuses. My wife can hear ten conversations going on at the same time. But not me. Not men. We hear one thing at a time. I'm convinced we're hindered through the lens of masculinity. I think it has something to do with the male chromosome missing that extra hearing mechanism. That's my theory.

Legalism works in much the same way. It's a narrow scope. It's a foggy lens—a lens that hinders true vision. It's like trying to drive a car with a foggy windshield. Dangerous. Treacherous.

Legalism fogs true vision. It makes Jesus look like a distorted, blurry figure—a pixilated pancake. Legalism made the religious leaders miss the obvious—that Jesus was the Messiah. Concern with every detail of the Law led the Jews to an unhealthy focus on their unrealistic idealism. For them, the Law was in crystal clear focus in the foreground, and Jesus was a blurry, unrecognizable figure in the background.

Feeding Your Appetite

What experiences have you had in your Christian life that others have dumped acid rain upon? How have you been the one dumping the rain?

Though we probably would never admit to having the type of legalistic attitude that emphasizes rules over people, if we're not careful we can lose sight of the infinite value that God places on human souls. List some ways that you can love the people around you today in the name of Jesus (i.e. your family, co-workers, classmates, neighbors).

How easy is it for the dos and don'ts of the Christian life to become your focus? How can you refocus on what really matters?

In what ways have you or are you trying to earn favor with God through your nice little checklist? When a checklist is your emphasis, how genuinely thriving is your relationship with Christ?

Your Discovery

6

To Whom Shall We Go?
John 6

"I stopped believing in Santa Claus when my mother took me to see him in a department store, and he asked for my autograph."
- Shirley Temple

Did you ever have those moments as a kid when you heard news so earth shattering and so unbelievable that it rocked the very foundation of everything you knew to be true of your world at the time? Maybe it was the unforgettable evening when your dad sat down with you and an illustrated storybook to explain to you how babies are made. Or maybe when you found out that *The Lion King* was *not* based on a true story. Or maybe when you discovered the truth about the Easter Bunny and Santa Claus. Or maybe when you first discovered that M&M's actually *do* melt in your hand. Or maybe when someone finally pointed out to you that you had been confusing *their* and *there* in anything you had ever written your entire life. Or maybe when you first heard the news that planes had wrecked into the Twin Towers in New York City or that a family member had passed away or someone you loved had cancer. Those moments are hard to hear, yet impossible to forget. We'd rather turn a deaf ear as if we heard nothing—as if nothing happened—as if our world had not just been turned upside down, even though our dangling, suspended, confused bodies tell us otherwise.

If you haven't noticed before now, Jesus often made statements that were (and are) pretty tough to swallow—both for His immediate audience and for us in the 21st century. He continuously confused and perplexed the religious leaders by challenging their interpretation of the Old Testament. He caused many to rethink everything they believed. He forced others to think outside of the little box in which they placed God. We saw it with Nicodemus. We saw it with the woman at the well. And now we see it again with some of Jesus' own disciples.

After performing the fourth sign in John, the feeding of the 5,000, Jesus took the opportunity, as He often did following a miracle, to chase a metaphor—to drive home a point—to connect a miracle involving bread and fish with the Bread of Life. He said,

> "I am *the living bread* that came down from heaven. If anyone eats of this bread he will live forever. The bread that I will give for the life of the world is My flesh" (John 6:51).

Much like Nicodemus and the Samaritan woman, Jesus' audience had a hard time understanding that He was speaking in spiritual terms rather than physical terms.[1] So it's not hard to see why some of His disciples responded the way they did:

> "Therefore, when many of His disciples heard this, they said, 'This teaching is hard! Who can accept it'" (John 6:60)?

Remember back in chapter two—the pseudo-believers? These were the same people. These were not the Twelve that Jesus was closest to. These were the *others*. The pseudo-disciples. And these guys missed the whole point of what Jesus was teaching.

What would be great is for us to read in the next few verses that the light came on for these disciples and they realized that Jesus was not actually instituting the ordinance of cannibalism. But the light never came on. Maybe you were confused here, as well. Eating people is bad, okay? Jesus—good. Cannibalism—bad. Let's get that straight before we move on.

Jesus, of course, was speaking in spiritual terms, not physical. But the pseudo-disciples missed the point. Their spiritual eyes were closed. They probably just stared blankly, not getting it—much like when I tell my son not to eat the newly discovered petrified dog poop in the backyard which he proudly holds high in the air like a priceless treasure. He doesn't understand. They didn't understand. And so we read what is arguably one of the saddest verses in Scripture, appropriately 6:66:

> "From that moment many of His disciples *turned back* and no longer accompanied Him."

Wow! They left. They fled. Deserted. Turned back. Went home. Had enough. Showed their true colors.

The Things Behind

A 2006 report revealed that over 8,000 U.S. volunteer military personnel have deserted since the war in Iraq began.[2] And no doubt there are hundreds more who have deserted since that report. But what does it mean to desert? It means to be A-WOL—Absent Without Leave. It means that a soldier makes a conscious choice to walk away from battle—to desert his fellow soldiers—to desert the cause—a selfish act of the will.

That's what these disciples did. With a conscious choice of their will, they packed up and ran from Jesus as fast as they could.

The word *turned back* in the original language literally means "to the things behind."[3] In other words, they went back to the very things they had left in order to follow Christ in the first place. Jesus' words in Luke 9:62 were meant for these types of deserters:

> "But Jesus said to him, 'No one who puts his hand to the plow and *looks back* is fit for the kingdom of God.'"

These guys were good at playing the game. They were good at following from a distance. They were good at playing the role of a disciple. But when the cost of discipleship got too tough, they hit the road. When they were too lazy to try to commit themselves to truly understanding Christ's teaching, they decided they'd rather go back to tax collecting, or studying in the synagogue, or shearing sheep, or catching delicious bass, or creating fashion designer yamikas, or changing the oil in Roman chariots or whatever it was they did before they followed Christ.

They went back to the things behind. The old way of life. The old habits. The old friends. The old routine. The old patterns. After seeing all the miracles. After witnessing a lame man walk. After joining in the feast of 5,000 men (probably close to 15,000 with women and children) from five slices of Wonderbread and two cans of Chicken of the Sea. After seeing the Messiah in all His glory, somehow the things behind were more appealing. The things behind were familiar. The things behind were easy. Jesus asked too much of them. His teachings were hard for them to understand. He probably hurt their feelings a few too many times. So they turned back. They found the nearest exit and got off the narrow road as quickly as possible.

Dietrich Bonhoeffer, a German theologian who suffered severely for his faith during the Jewish Holocaust, said this regarding the road that true disciples travel:

> The road of the disciples is narrow. It is easy to go past it; it is easy to miss it; it is easy to lose it, even for those who have already walked it. It is hard to find. The path is narrow indeed; there is a real danger of falling off on both sides.[4]

That's what happened to these guys. They walked the narrow road for a while. But danger came. The road got hard. The road became difficult. And they preferred the broader road. Maybe you've considered the same thing—that it would just be easier to get off now while you can—that you'd have less to explain to your friends and your family if you got off—that you might have a better chance to get in that fraternity if you got off—that you might get a promotion at work if you got off—that you could run back to those sexual habits if you got off—that you could visit those websites again if you got off—that you could cut or starve yourself again if you got off. Has the road gotten hard? Too narrow for you?

It's no wonder Jesus turned to the Twelve and asked,

"You don't want to go away too, do you" (6:67)?

I absolutely love Peter's response:

"Lord *who will we go to*? You have the words of eternal life" (6:68).

Jesus, the Son of God, the Living Christ, possesses the words of eternal life—words that alone have the power to save, heal and forgive. He is the Bread of Life, the Manna from Heaven, the Living Water, the Narrow Gate, the King of Kings and Lord of Lords. Peter understood this. Who will we go to? Will we go back wasting our lives on temporal things? Who else can speak the world and endless galaxies into existence? Who else can calm the storm with only a whisper? Who else can restore the human soul and reunite it with the Living God who created it? Who else but the Bread of Life can satisfy the spiritual hunger of every man and woman? Who? Who? Who? Peter found Him and held on with all of his might. Others found Him and then let Him go.

> The only thing that matters is finding (Jesus). If we know that, then we will walk the narrow way to life through the narrow gate of the cross of Jesus Christ, then the narrowness of the way itself will reassure us.[5]

The Discovery: Beyond the Jesus of Flapjacks and Grilled Cheese

Feeding Your Appetite

If Jesus posed that same question to you ("You don't want to go away too do you?"), what would be your honest response?

How do you feel when you hear about a soldier deserting? How does that compare to how you feel when you hear about a "Christian" turning his back on Christ?

What hard-to-understand concepts about the Christian faith have been challenging for you?

If you have contemplated turning back "to the things behind," what caused you to have these thoughts? Talk openly to God and tell Him how you feel. Read Proverbs 3:5-6 and ask the Holy Spirit to keep your steps on the narrow path.

The Discovery: Beyond the Jesus of Flapjacks and Grilled Cheese

Your Discovery

7

Identity Crisis – Part 1
John 7

"God … is to be sought by His saints in the hours of early morning but condescends to seek out even sinners at dusk and washes them at evening in the peace of His presence and throws round their shoulders the cloak of His acceptance and puts on their fingers the ring of His pleasure."
- Rich Mullins

Every artist has his influences—his inspiration—his heroes. Rich Mullins is one of mine. Rich's music had an enormous impact on my life as a young songwriter and worship leader. He wrote and sang about Christ as if He was the one, all-consuming passion of his life—as if his relationship with Jesus was thriving, growing and flourishing.

Tragically, Rich died on September 19, 1997, in an automobile accident, but his music and legacy live on. He helped to shape the landscape of the early Contemporary Christian Music industry in a profound way. He defied and challenged traditional taboos, often playing concerts barefooted wearing simply a t-shirt and torn jeans. His lyrics were passionate, frank and honest, openly describing personal and spiritual struggles in his search to know God more intimately.

What I love most about Rich's legacy was the fact that, in the midst of all of his successes and accomplishments, he never ceased to keep Jesus Christ and the Gospel his central focus. He once commented:

> Sometimes it concerns me, the number of people who can quote my songs, or they can quote the songs of several people, but they can't quote the Scriptures—as if anything a musician might have to say would be worth listening to ... If you want entertainment, I suggest Christian entertainment, because I think it's good. But if you want spiritual nourishment, I suggest you go to church or read your Bible.[1]

Rich never wavered in preaching the fundamentals of the Christian faith through his music. Scripture was the most important thing to Rich. In one of his most famous and emotionally powerful songs, "Creed," Rich took the *Apostles' Creed*, the most fundamentally orthodox statement of the Christian faith, and put a melody to it. In this song he drew a line in the sand declaring,

> I believe in God the Father, Almighty Maker of Heaven and Maker of Earth, And in Jesus Christ His only begotten Son, our Lord. He was conceived of the Holy Spirit, Born of the Virgin Mary, Suffered under Pontius Pilate. He was crucified and dead and buried. And I believe what I believe is what makes me what I am. I did not make it, no it is making me. It is the very truth of God and not the invention of any man.[2]

Rich was committed to the basic truths of Christianity—the truth about Jesus Christ—that He came as the Messiah of the world to live, to die, to atone for sin and to rise again conquering death and offering new life. Jesus Christ is the only hope for the world. If you haven't picked up on this as a major theme of this book, and a major theme of the book of John, you're missing it. John intentionally reiterated it over and over again—that Jesus is the Christ—the greatest possible discovery known to man. It never gets old to me—the fact that Christ came to this earth for helpless, sinful human beings. That's the only message that will last through eternity. That's the only message that ultimately matters.

In John 7, this fundamental doctrine of Christianity is questioned yet again—the doctrine of Christ—that Christ is the Messiah, the Son of God, God in human flesh.

The setting is the Feast of Tabernacles in Jerusalem—a Jewish festival requiring all males living within twenty miles of the city to attend—a festival of numerous ritualistic activities involving water.[3] Jesus showed up secretly halfway through the feast and began teaching about the Living Water—a subject that His audience would have instantly connected back to the festival rituals—an easy visual aid. But His secret lasted about as long as a twinkie in the hand of my two-year-old. Try as He may to stay under the radar, whenever Jesus taught, the masses flocked. The vultures swarmed. The flamingos committeed. You get the picture.

As He taught, the crowds were amazed. Big surprise. As usual, He stunned the religious leaders with His knowledge and they remarked,

"How does He know the Scriptures, since He hasn't been trained" (John 7:15)?

They missed one itty bitty, teensy weensy detail. *Jesus is God.* And as Jesus taught, Scripture says that the crowds became divided in their opinions about Him (v. 43). They all had varying ideas about Jesus' true identity. Let's take a look at some of these opinions.

A Total Loony

Jesus' own brothers fall into this category. In a mocking tone, they said,

> "Go to Judea so Your disciples can see Your works that You are doing. For no one does anything in secret while he's seeking public recognition ... (For *not even His brothers believed* in Him ...)" (John 7:3-5).

Ouch! Not even His brothers believed Him. Instead they mocked. During the festivals of that time period, false messiahs came out of the woodwork. They entered the crowded city teaching strange ideas and trying to gain a following. So Jesus' brothers were literally saying, "Go show off your messiah skills like all the other false messiahs at the festival and see who you can impress." Their unbelief is felt in their sarcasm.

The Prophet

Others believed that Jesus was the Prophet (v. 40)—a nice way of lending some credibility and authority to Jesus. It was probably more of a kind gesture to those who felt sorry for His delusional dreams of grandeur. And they failed to connect the dots with Jesus as both the Prophet and the Messiah.

The Messiah

Just like we've seen before, some of the crowd believed that Jesus was the actual Messiah (v. 41), after all,

> "No man ever spoke like this" (John 7:46)!

But we are left wondering whether their belief was genuine or whether they were simply impressed by His rhetoric and magic tricks, missing the point.

A Wannabe

Then there were others who were just ignorant of the facts and assumed He was a wannabe. They said,

"Surely the Messiah doesn't come from Galilee, does He? *Doesn't the Scripture say* that the Messiah comes from David's offspring and from the town of Bethlehem" (John 7:41-42)?

Umm, yea. It does. And if I'm not mistaken, wasn't Jesus born in Bethlehem and wasn't He from the lineage of David? Yea. He was.

Ignorant! This crowd suffered from a bad case of the stupids and were too lazy to look into the facts about Jesus.

All of this is neatly laid out for us and put into nice little categories, but it means nothing unless we put it into our context. So what about us? What about you? The crowd had a million different opinions and conceptions about Jesus. What's yours?

Chances are if you've read this far in the book, you are a follower of Christ seeking to live your life for His glory. If not, thanks for being honest! I'm glad you're still reading. Maybe you've found yourself falling into one of the categories above. Maybe you think that Jesus was a psycho—a total loony—a man in need of an enlightening conversation with Dr. Phil. Or maybe you find yourself feeling sorry for Jesus and His fanatical dreams. Or maybe if you were truly honest with yourself you'd have to say that you've never really looked into the cold hard facts about Jesus. Maybe you're still trying to figure all of this out, and that's all right. My prayer for you is that you would continue to seek the truth in your journey toward God and make the personal decision to follow Christ as I explained in chapter one.

But as you continue this journey toward your discovery, remember this: The claims Jesus made cannot be attributed to merely a good teacher alone. Based upon the claims He made, He has to be more than a moral instructor. Here's what C.S. Lewis said about this:

I am trying here to prevent anyone saying the really foolish thing that people often say about Him: "I'm ready to accept Jesus as a great moral teacher, but I don't accept His claim to be God." That is one thing we must not say. A man who was merely a man and said the sort of things Jesus said would not be a great moral teacher. He would either be a lunatic—on a level with the man who says he is a poached egg—or else he would be the Devil of Hell. You must make your choice. Either this man was, and is, the Son of God; or else a madman or something worse. You can shut Him up for a fool, you can spit at Him and kill Him as a demon; or you can fall at His feet and call Him Lord and God. But let us not come with any patronizing nonsense about His being a great human teacher. He has not left that open to us. He did not intend to.[4]

Good stuff, Clive! But what about those of us who *do* believe that Jesus is who He said He was? Are there other categories that we might fall into? Is it possible we could be a follower of Christ and still have the wrong perception about the identity of Jesus? Absolutely. So hang with me and we'll look at some of those misconceptions in the next chapter.

Feeding Your Appetite

What other opinions have you heard regarding the identity of Jesus? And how do these opinions conflict with what Scripture claims about Jesus?

The Discovery: Beyond the Jesus of Flapjacks and Grilled Cheese

If you were one of Jesus' brothers who grew up under the same roof, what would it take for you to believe in Him? Why do you think it took more convincing for His own brothers?

What difference does it make if Jesus was just a great moral teacher, but perhaps just had some of His facts mixed up? Why does C.S. Lewis say that the great moral teacher option is a "really foolish thing"?

Your Discovery

8

Identity Crisis – Part 2
John 8

"Well, when I bumped into her, she clanged. And little old ladies ought never to clang!"
- Andy Griffith

There's no feeling that leaves you quite as vulnerable and helpless as having your identity stolen. A few weeks ago this happened to me. The sad part is, it wasn't stolen. I gave it away. Like a bumbling idiot I gift-wrapped my identity and merrily handed it to a zit-faced hacker sitting in his mom's basement. To my credit, the e-mail looked legitimate—the famous last words of many a victim of ID theft. But it did! It was two days before Christmas and I received one of those mass phishing e-mails that looked identical to other PayPal e-mails that I occasionally receive. I followed through with it, thinking that I was doing my duty as a privileged PayPal customer.

The instant I clicked *send* on the form I knew I had made a mistake. Call it instinct. Call it Firefox instantaneously popping up a bright red warning box with flashing skulls and slogans like "Death to the passerby" and "You idiot, you just funded a nuclear warhead aimed at a small island!"

"Wonderful," I thought. *"It'll arrive just in time for Christmas!"* I held myself close and rocked in the fetal position in the corner of the room.

I gave the world my identity—everything about me—everything important—all of it. It was out there—every bit of it. Nothing hidden. That's exactly what John wanted. That's what he wanted people to know about Jesus—everything. Nothing hidden. No misconceptions. This was his number one goal—that no one misses the real identity of Jesus—the ultimate discovery. This was his number one concern—more than my concern that America never loses its love and admiration for The Andy Griffith Show in the wake of reality TV and the I-bet-you-can't-out-do-this-one mentality of television programming—more than my concern that brown sugar and cinnamon Pop Tarts never go out of production—more than my concern that my kids understand that running around naked in our house is cool, but not so much out in public, and not so much fifteen years from now—more than my concern that my kids never take up playing in traffic as an extreme sport—and more than my concern that my kids never know or at very least never speak the name of the purple singing monstrosity *Barney* in our house as long as I live. As passionate as I am about those things, John was even more passionate about communicating Jesus' true identity.

Over and over he reiterated this one essential truth. Again and again John drove home the point that Jesus is the Christ, the prophesied Messiah. And more than that, that Jesus is God wrapped in human flesh.

John 8:58 is a crucial verse in John's depiction and increasing awareness of who Jesus is:

"Jesus said to them, 'I assure you: Before Abraham was, *I am.*'"

This is one of the clearest arguments for the deity of Jesus in the entire Bible. By using the title *I AM*, Jesus very clearly claimed to be God. He claimed for Himself the divine title found throughout the Old Testament. When Moses asked God what name He should use in defending his authority before pharaoh, God simply said, "I AM WHO I AM" (Exodus 3:14). I love Louie Giglio's explanation of *I AM:*

> It's an amazing name. In Hebrew the word for *I AM* is *Hayah*. *Hayah* carries with it the idea of the very breath of God. In English the name *I AM* translates into the verb *to be*. Or simply *be*. Therefore God's name is *Be. I AM – I Be. I AM* is the present tense, active form of the verb to be. As God's name, it declares that He is unchanging, constant, unending, always present, always God.[1]

That's an amazing title. Think of *I AM* as one of the top steps in a series of escalating stairs—the lower steps being titles that we've already looked at, the Living Water and the Bread of Life. John escalated to a breaking point—*I AM*. Now there was no doubt to anyone in earshot of Jesus that He was claiming to be God.

I love it. I love that this is the title by which God chose to reveal Himself to Moses—the unchanging God—the always-present God—always there by Moses' side. The always-existing One knew Moses—in the same way Jesus knew Nathaniel before they ever met (John 1:48)—in the same way Jesus knew the Samaritan woman with all of the baggage of her past (John 4:29)—in the same way Jesus knows you and everything about you—every detail, every mistake, every thought, every action, every intention. Jesus knows. Jesus knows *you*.

Here's a fundamental truth that we can't afford to miss.

Our identity as followers of Christ is totally wrapped up in Christ's identity.

In other words, Christ is our life (Col. 3:4). So the converse must also be true. Our misconceptions of Jesus misconstrue or blur our identity as followers of Christ. In my experience, there are at least two misconceptions about Christ that most Christ-followers believe at some point in their relationship with Him. So I want to clear these up briefly.

Misconception #1: "Jesus is my Homeboy"

The homeboy mentality says this: Since Jesus is my best friend, He'll let me do whatever I want, and He'll always be there to forgive me when I mess up. The homeboy mentality makes Jesus nothing more than a confession box that I spill my guts to once I mess up. It views Jesus as a passive parent, like the mom from *Gilmore Girls*—the idea that I can mess around with my boyfriend or girlfriend, masturbate, view internet porn and repeatedly push the boundaries of right and wrong simply because I know Jesus will always forgive me. It's the idea that I have an endless supply of get-out-of-jail-free cards—since Jesus is one of the guys I can sin as much as I want and simply ask for forgiveness because He understands how I really am anyway. But Romans 6:1-2 says just the opposite:

> "What should we say then? Should we continue in sin in order that grace may multiply? Absolutely not! How can we who died to sin still live in it?"

And here's the resulting identity of the follower of Christ who falls prey to this misconception.

The Cheap Grace Identity

The cheap grace identity laughs in Jesus' face as the blood flows down from the cross. The cheap grace identity says, "Jesus, thanks for dying for my sin so that I can mess up as many times as I want and not really feel bad about it since you paid for it all anyway!" It says to Jesus, "Jesus, thanks for caring enough for me that You would let massive spikes be driven through your hands into a wooden beam so that I can use my hands to get in my girlfriend's pants!" The cheap grace identity is nothing more than a cheap imitation for coward Christians.

Misconception #2: "Jesus is a Tyrant"

The tyrant mentality is the polar opposite. It says this: "Since Jesus hates sin and especially hates when *I* sin, He is up there in heaven somewhere waiting for me to mess up again so that He can slap another ticket on the windshield of my life." The tyrant mentality views Jesus as the cop with the chip on His shoulder, like the Jack Bauer of heaven—the rogue agent out for revenge waiting for His next victim to slip up. And here's the resulting identity.

The Legalism Identity

The believer who lives by this misconception lives in fear. As we talked about in chapter five, legalism shadows Jesus' real identity. But not only that, it shadows the identity of the follower of Christ. It says that I must live in worry that I haven't done *enough* to *please* God and I've done *too much* to *displease* God. Having an identity of legalism means that I must live by a list of dos and don'ts. I must cross all my *T*'s, dot all my *I*'s, read ten chapters in my Bible everyday, pray three hours, witness to at least thirty people a day, eat my greens, recycle my cans, cover my mouth when I sneeze, don't kick the cat, bla bla bla. Not that any of those things are wrong. But it's the attitude that accompanies the actions that make them wrong.

What's wrong is when I think that what I do earns me points with God, or helps to reduce the demerits I have with God. What's wrong is when, out of a sense of *duty*, I help an old lady carry her groceries while all along envisioning the Jack Bauer God peering overhead. Here's what John said about living in fear:

> "There is *no fear in love*; instead, perfect love drives out fear, because fear involves punishment" (1 John 4:18).

Did you catch that? That is the right conception about God. Fear is driven out when God's love is brought in. So here it is.

The Right Conception: Jesus is *I AM*

The *I AM* Jesus *is* perfect love. The *I AM* Jesus has always been and always will be. The *I AM* Jesus loves sinners, and judges sin. The *I AM* Jesus is both a forgiving God, and a just judge. The *I AM* Jesus spoke the world into existence and breathed the breath of life into every human being. The *I AM* Jesus bore the sin of the world on His body and bruised the body of His One and Only Son at the same time. The *I AM* Jesus felt both the rejection of God on the cross and the unbearable turning away of His own face from His Son. The *I AM* Jesus was prophesied by men of God and created the very breath of the prophets who spoke the words. The *I AM* Jesus is both transcendent and immanent—He is holy and far removed, yet He is personal and very near to His children. The *I AM* Jesus revolutionizes the identity of His followers.

The True Follower Identity

The true follower identity says that because Jesus suffered for my sins, I want to live my life for Him simply because I love Him—not from a sense of obligation—not from a sense fear—not because He forces my hand—not because I think I can earn more God-points. No. Only because I love Him. And since He gave His life for me, the least that I can do is live for Him. The true follower identity is totally wrapped up in the identity of Christ, the *I AM*, the never-changing, always-present Maker of the universe. That's the identity that I want to be true of my life. I hope you can say the same.

"If you continue in My word, you really are My disciples. You will know the truth, and the truth will set you free" (John 8:31-32).

Now, I'm gonna go rest in *I AM,* watch Andy Griffith and try to forget that I helped finance terrorism.

Feeding Your Appetite

How has Jesus proved Himself to You as *I AM*? In other words, how does your perception of Him as *I AM*, the always-existing One, move you into greater worship of Him as He moves and works in your life?

How would you rate your identity as a Christ-follower?

CheapGrace	True Follower	Legalism
Homeboy	*I AM*	*Tyrant*

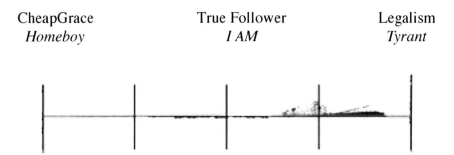

What are some specific ways that You have been guilty of having the homeboy misconception (treating God's forgiveness lightly) or the tyrant misconception (driven by fear more than love)?

The Discovery: Beyond the Jesus of Flapjacks and Grilled Cheese

How does having the right conception of God affect the way you view your own identity in Christ?

Spend a few moments thanking God, the *I AM,* for the intimate relationship that He makes available to you through His Son Jesus Christ.

Your Discovery

9

The Problem of Evil as it Relates to Chick-fil-A Cows
John 9

"Smoking kills. If you're killed, you've lost a very important part of your life."
- Brooke Shields, during an interview to become spokesperson for a federal anti-smoking campaign

I make some pretty dumb statements much of the time. One of my dumbest verbal blunders is becoming an unfortunate, frequent event, almost a habit, if you will. Once the conversation heads this direction, you can predict the outcome like you can predict how Bill Gates would fare in the Ironman World Triathlon. So off I go with diarrhea of the mouth falling headfirst into my own conversation trap over and over again. Maybe it's happened to you and that would make me feel a little better. Here's how it usually goes.

I'll be small talking with a friend or acquaintance when his or her parents happen by. With total sincerity and goodwill, I'll say something like, "Hey, introduce me to your grandparents!" And my conversation buddy will consequently respond with awkward tone, "Actually these are my parents!" Since saving face is out of the question, I'll usually follow that up with another brainless statement about the aging process and the effects of global warming. Every now and then, when God decides to smile down on my pathetic condition, I'll actually shut my mouth.

Jesus' disciples make me feel better about myself in that specific area. All through the gospels they consistently insert their feet into their oral cavity—arguing about who should be the greatest in the kingdom of heaven (Matt. 18:1, Mark 9:33-34, Luke 9:46), who should sit next to Jesus in heaven (Matt. 20:21), who should get to live the longest (John 21:20-23), rebuking little kids for cuddling with Jesus (Mark 10:13), and the list goes on and on. I'm forever puzzled by such displays.

What really baffles me, though, is Jesus' continued patience with them. You never see Jesus muttering under His breath about the moronic thing Peter just said. You never overhear Jesus talking with John the Baptist about possibly trading out some of His dumber disciples with John's. He's forever patient.

John 9:2 is a verse that, at least at first glance, appears to be a classic foot-in-mouth scenario for the disciples. In fact, I've heard many preachers and teachers say that. I used to think that. But as I think through the bigger picture of where the disciples may have been coming from, I now think otherwise. Let's look at the text:

> "As He was passing by, He saw a man blind from birth. His disciples questioned Him: 'Rabbi, who sinned, this man or his parents, that he was born blind'" (John 9:1-2)?

Wow! Loaded question! Jesus answered them not only verbally, but also physically with a miracle—the sixth sign in John. He healed the blind man, displaying the awesome power and hand of God to everyone watching. John's consistent use of light imagery ties everything together. In John 1 we saw that Jesus is the Light who came into the darkness. In John 9 Jesus was, in a practical sense, the Light to a blind man born into darkness. John was intentional about the accounts of Jesus' life that he included, and he packaged it in a way that is thoroughly consistent.

According to Jesus, the man was born blind so that God's power could be displayed on his behalf. His condition had nothing to do with *his* sin or his *parents'* sin. Jesus was showing off God's power, plain and simple. And the man became a walking testimony to the power of God.

The Reason for the Question

But what about the disciples' question? What was going on in their minds that they would ask a question like this? Well, here's a quick rundown on what they were probably thinking. They may have been thinking about Exodus 34:6-7 that says,

> "Yahweh is a compassionate and gracious God . . . but He will not leave the guilty unpunished, bringing the consequences of the father's wrongdoing *on the children and grandchildren* to the third and fourth generation."

And they may have been thinking of 2 Samuel 12 where David's adultery resulted in the death of his son. These passages and others like it were certainly looming in the disciples' heads, and legitimately so. That's why I don't think their question was so idiotic after all. And chances are, you've asked similar questions as you've witnessed the cruelty and evil in the world.

The other day Tasha and I received a phone call from two girls that were in my former youth ministry. They were asking this same question and it went something like this: "We were studying 2 Samuel 12 in Sunday school and we have to know something. Are children punished for the sins of their parents?" This happens to be a perfect icebreaker for parties, by the way. Try it sometime.

I told them to go ask their pastor. Actually, no, I did manage to stumble through a response, but since then I've ironed it out a bit.

Still, it's an issue that I don't claim to have all figured out, and I humbly hold to my position.

Let's have a look at the passage the girls referred to. 2 Samuel 12 describes the unfortunate result of David's sin of adultery with Bathsheba. She had consequently gotten pregnant and given birth to a son. We pick up in verse fifteen where Scripture says,

"the Lord *struck* the child and he became ill."

A couple of verses later we discover that the child passed away. So apparently, God killed David's son because of David's sin. This doesn't sound like the heart-warming God we have come to know and love. And there's no getting around the fact that this is a tough issue, but one that deserves a response. So here we go.

1. God's divine actions are spoken of in human terms.

As readers of Scripture, we have to understand that "the Bible gives a varied portrait of the nature of God."[1] What do I mean? Imagine that you're watching an artist paint a beautiful canvass. As he makes delicate strokes, you are seeing the whole thing come together stroke by stroke. But until it's completed, you only see the individual, varied portions of it. Once it is completed, you see the whole picture. That's what I think is going on here with David's son. God's actions are described as *striking* because it is the best way to humanly understand what happened. We see God's *divine* actions from a *human* standpoint.

Here's another example that might help. Exodus 32 describes an event that raises very similar questions. If you grew up in Sunday school, you might remember Exodus 32 as the golden calf episode. Remember? Rather than worshiping God, His people decided it would be cool to worship a pimped out Chick-fil-A mascot. So God told Moses He was going to destroy *everyone* for the sin of idolatry. Moses pleaded with God to change His mind and guess what? ... God did.

"The Lord *changed His mind* about the disaster He said He would bring to His people" (Exodus 32:14).

He what? He changed His mind? He acted differently than originally planned? He hadn't really made up His mind after all? He didn't really know what He was going to do? He can be coerced and manipulated?

At first glance, yes. But this is where we have to understand that we see only one part of the whole portrait.

Scripture is speaking of God in human terms—anthropomorphic terms to be exact. By saying, "The Lord changed His mind," Scripture describes God's actions in very human terms that can be easily understood. So it's not as if God didn't know He would make that choice. We're at the mercy of human analogy here. Thomas Aquinas, a 13th century theologian, made the point early on in Christian history that we are incredibly limited in human language to describe God and His actions. The reason for this? "All words used of God come from creatures."[2]

He's exactly right and this passage illustrates our limited understanding as well as our limited view of this portrait. But I think there's a second and probably better answer to all of this.

2. What does the totality of Scripture teach?

A fundamental principle of biblical interpretation says that you cannot take one verse of Scripture and build an entire theology (what you believe about God) upon it. You always weigh and balance Scripture with Scripture. Obviously, we don't have the space or time to examine *everything* the Bible teaches on this subject. But let's at least look at a few passages.

Deuteronomy 24:16 says,

"Fathers are not to be put to death for their children or children for their fathers; each person will be put to death *for his own sin.*"

Seems straightforward. Kids should not be punished for their parents' sins. Got it. But as we saw earlier, Exodus 34:7 says differently:

"But He (God) will not leave the guilty unpunished, bringing the consequences of the fathers' wrongdoing *on the children and grandchildren* to the third and fourth generation."

Now, we've balanced and it appears that we've gotten nowhere. Is there anything else that can help us? Yep. Let's back up and look at the full context of Exodus 34:

"Yahweh is a compassionate and gracious God, slow to anger and *rich in faithful love* and truth, maintaining faithful love to a thousand generations, forgiving wrongdoing, rebellion, and sin" (Exodus 34:6).

The word for *faithful love* in the Hebrew is one word that means to have unconditional love regardless of the actions of the individual. Regardless of the sin of your parents or grandparents, God still loves them and forgives them. And He doesn't hold *you* responsible. Regardless of your own sin, He will forever love you with faithful, unchanging love that never lets go. And notice how long this love endures—not just for three or four generations, but for a *thousand* generations. That's a poetic way of screaming in all caps, *FOREVER!* The reality is this:

Faithful love does not execute arbitrary punishment on the innocent.

When I look at the totality of Scripture in its full context, that's the conclusion I come to. But I also have a third response.

3. The word *consequences* is more appropriate than *punishment*.

There's a little key word in Exodus 34:7 that I glossed over a minute ago. *Consequences*—an incredibly important word for this discussion. In Hebrew, it's the word *Awon* and it's often used interchangeably in the Old Testament with the word *punishment*. The difference is, it's not punishment as we tend to think of punishment. When we think of punishment, we naturally infer that there must be someone *inflicting* the punishment. In Hebrew, the focus is not the *punisher*, but the *receiver*. The focus is not God. Nor is it His punishing actions. Instead, the focus is the responsibility of the guilty party. The focus is the *result* of the sin.[3] That's why *consequences* is a better word. It clarifies the focus. That clarity is this:

Consequences involve the removal of God's protective hand from the effects of sin.

So let's be realistic for a minute. We live in a messed up world where the consequences for sin often affect more than one person. Turn on the evening news for five minutes and you'll discover this to be true. That's the world we live in. If you decide to drink and drive, you may kill yourself or someone else. You may even walk away from the mangled mass of metal without a scratch, while the mini-van full of dead children will forever remind you of the consequences for your sin. The grim reality is, there are consequences for our sin that often carry on to affect our children and our grandchildren, our friends and relatives.

I have a friend who recently had a baby that was born with a hole in her heart because my friend chose to use drugs during her pregnancy. She'll have to live with that the rest of her life—both the mother and the baby. So should we say that God is the author of the sick evil that happened to this precious little girl?

Absolutely not! To say that God is the creator of the evil and wickedness in the world is a grave error. Yes, God is sovereign (in complete control) over all of the affairs of men and nothing happens outside the realm of His control, but He sometimes allows the workings of men to reach their fullest and often grossest potential because He has given them the freedom of choice (i.e. The Holocaust). Understand that there are consequences for our sin that sometimes carry on to our children or grandchildren. But God, in no way, arbitrarily punishes or judges His precious children for the sins of another. We must always make that distinction.

Just to recap: We'll never be able to fully describe the ways of God within the limits of human language, we must always read Scripture in its fullest context, and we should always make the distinction between consequences and punishment. So, no, I don't blame the disciples for their question.

Feeding Your Appetite

What specific evil in the world or in your life situation has caused you to doubt God's love for humanity or His sovereign power over all things?

Have you noticed any consequences of your own sin and choices that have carried down to someone else?

Knowing that God is not the author of evil but that He does allow the consequences of our choices to take effect, what specific steps will you take to make wise choices that honor Him?

Recommended Reading:

Where is God? A Personal Story of Finding God in Grief and Suffering by John Feinberg

Your Discovery

10

God Loves Dumb Animals
John 10

"Prone to wander, Lord I feel it, prone to leave the God I love."
- Robert Robinson, "Come Thou Fount of Every Blessing"

There is no metaphor to describe Jesus that intrigues me more than one of the metaphors found in John 10—the Good Shepherd. It's an amazing title when all of the cultural blanks are filled in. Our culture knows very little about shepherding. But it's a concept that Jesus' audience would have been very familiar with. It's one filled with beauty, love, tenderness and compassion.

One of the first verses of Scripture that I ever memorized was from Psalm 23. Actually, it was the whole chapter. Earlier I mentioned my mom's fanaticism with Scripture memory. Psalm 23 is one of those that she forced Smooth and me to memorize one day before Dad got home from the office. She wanted to impress him with our unlikely abilities. I suggested a different skill to show off instead—Smooth's newly discovered ninja jack-in-the-box routine that involved my uncanny ability to twist and contort his wiry frame enough to squeeze him down inside of our toy box. But Mom wouldn't have it. For several hours we sat on the couch as she withheld lunch and snack time until we had progressed a certain length in the chapter. And when Dad got home, we obediently (and robotically) spouted it out like we were made for the moment. As soon as we were done, Smooth and I made a mad dash for the woods like a rat pouncing on a cheeto. Mom and Dad were both proud. When I think back to days like that, it makes me thankful for godly parents who taught us to love Jesus and to love His Word. I think that's why Psalm 23 has always been so special to me.

There are numerous parallels between Jesus' discourse about the Good Shepherd and Psalm 23. No doubt as Jesus taught, His hearers immediately thought of the twenty-third Psalm. The imagery, the wording, the mental pictures—there is a definite connection. As we move through this chapter, I'll point out a few of those connections.

Notice how Jesus began:

"I am the *good shepherd*. The good shepherd lays down his life for the sheep" (John 10:11).

That right there is amazing to me. The Good Shepherd does what? He lays down His life. For who? For the sheep—sheep that are unquestionably the dumbest creatures to ever roam the planet. You've probably heard some of this before, but let me just quickly summarize some verified facts about sheep.

Their brains are tiny. They can't get up if they fall over. They often wander off from the rest of the flock and get lost. They are utterly defenseless against wild animals. They have no sense of direction. They will walk right off of a cliff if given the opportunity. I could go on and on. And what amazes me is that Jesus said that He lays down His very *life* for the sheep—a slightly unbalanced tradeoff. We are the sheep—people created in His image—people who continually wander—people who are dumb. Last week I got mad at my wife

The Discovery: Beyond the Jesus of Flapjacks and Grilled Cheese

because I stayed up too late and ate too many doughnuts and it made me irritable. I'm dumb. Yet, Jesus the Good Shepherd loves me. He loves you. He loves us in spite of us—in spite of our stupidity. Let's dive in a little deeper and look at some of these characteristics.

We Wander

Sheep wander. They are directionally challenged. And so are we. We wander off the path. We get lost.

Everybody has a story about how when they were a kid they wandered away from their mom at the mall, or the supermarket or wherever and they were lost for a period of time and they wet their pants, bla bla bla. My story isn't that great. It's very anticlimactic, to say the least. But my middle brother, Heelz[1], has an amazing story! At least I think it's amazing. When he was about three-years-old he got lost on the *sidewalk* of our church where my dad was the pastor. That's right. Right there on the church sidewalk, twenty yards from where my mom was jawing it up inside, he was lost. He cried, panicked, and cried some more. For about thirty minutes this went on until someone figured out what was going on. Was he really lost? Of course not. He was standing on the church sidewalk. Completely safe! Completely *not* lost! But in *his* mind he was. He got disoriented. It was dark. He lost his bearings. He wandered off from the group, the surroundings looked different and he had no idea where he was.

That's exactly how we are as God's sheep. We wander just far enough to freak out. We wander off just enough to become disoriented and think that God has forgotten us. But that's what I love about our Good Shepherd. He gently redirects our steps onto the right path.

> "He renews my life; He leads me along *the right paths* for
> His names' sake" (Psalm 23:3).

When the scars of sin and the world take their toll, He gently leads us back on the right path. Roy Hession, a great preacher of another generation, said this about our wandering:

We may, and sometimes do, slip off the Highway, for it is narrow. One little step aside and we are off the path and in darkness. It is always because of a failure in obedience somewhere or a failure to be weak enough to let God do all.[2]

The path is treacherous for sheep. Sheep aren't good on their feet. The road is narrow. But we have a Good Shepherd who gently leads—who kindly leads. Even through the darkest valley the Shepherd is there (Ps. 23:4). Again, Roy Hession:

As I crawl up again to the Highway on hands and knees, I come again to Him and His blood for cleansing. Jesus is waiting there to fill my cup to overflowing once again.[3]

The Good Shepherd is waiting to receive us again—to help us walk the path He has laid out. He waits there to clean us off and restore us once again. Is there sin in your own life that you need cleansing from? Can you point back to a time where you got off the path because of jealousy or anger or when you stayed up too late eating doughnuts? Maybe it was when you flew off the handle at your parents because they read your e-mail? But if you had nothing to hide you wouldn't be so upset, right? Wherever you may have exited the path, the Shepherd is waiting to bring you back, to restore you and to lead you on.

We Starve

This is the most intriguing thing to me about sheep—they actually have to be taught to eat and drink. Will Womble, a real-life shepherd, had this to say about what he observed in his early days of shepherding:

The first thing the sheep taught us was that they have to be taught, they don't naturally know how to take care of themselves. That first winter ... they began to starve to death with lots of hay and sweet feed available. We soon learned that they needed to be taught to eat.[4]

Wow! That's hard for me to imagine. We sure didn't have to teach my son how to eat. He pretty much came out of the womb gobbling up the afterbirth! But remember, sheep are dumb. And so are we. Our Shepherd must continually teach us and re-teach us until we get it. Psalm 23 reminds us of this same truth:

"He lets me lie down in green pastures; He leads me beside *quiet waters*" (Psalm 23:2).

Honestly, I always used to think that this verse had something to do with taking a nap—I think because Smooth and I used to listen to a random nature sounds CD at night to go to sleep to. Birds chirping. Rain and thunder. A trickling stream. A crocodile devouring a seal. Pleasant sounds like that. So whenever I read, "He leads me beside still waters" I assumed the Psalmist was ready for naptime.

But what he's actually saying is, "My Shepherd leads me to the waters because I'm too dumb to find it on my own. I would die of thirst if He didn't lead me there." That's the idea here. As our Shepherd, He has to continually lead us back to the stream and back to the hay where we can drink and eat—where we can find refreshment—where He can restore our soul. That's what it means to be dependent. That's what our Good Shepherd does for us. He teaches. He trains. And if we're too stubborn to listen, we starve to death.

We Recognize

This last trait is a positive one. Sheep know the voice of their master. As dumb as they are in other areas, they are keenly familiar with the voice of the shepherd. This is critical. Jesus said,

"The sheep follow him (the shepherd) because *they recognize* his voice" (John 10:4b).

Sheep that are well acquainted with the voice of the shepherd will never run to another. There is never a competition for what shepherd can gather the most. The real shepherd wins every time. How familiar are you with the voice of *your* Shepherd? Does His voice wake you up every morning with the thrill of living another day for His glory? Is His Word taking root in your heart so as to filter out the competing voices and calls of false shepherds in the world? Are the messages that are being sent out from the media and pop culture drowning out the voice of your Good Shepherd? The reality is, when the voice of our Shepherd becomes dull and hard to ascertain, the problem lies with us, not with our Shepherd. His voice is steady. His voice never falters. Listen for it afresh today. Ask Him to speak clearly to you today. He probably already has.

Lord, tune our hearts to hear your voice and obey.

Feeding Your Appetite

How do you find it applicable to your own life that Scripture speaks of your relationship to God like that of a sheep to its shepherd?

How have you found yourself imitating the behavior of sheep in your relationship with God? Wandering? Starving? Etc.

The Discovery: Beyond the Jesus of Flapjacks and Grilled Cheese

What competing voices are calling for your attention?

If you have extra time, read Psalm 23 and write down a few of your own observations.

Your Discovery

11

A Boy and Three Bears: A Parable About Faith and Doubt
John 11

"People have this obsession. They want you to be like you were in 1969. They want you to, because otherwise their youth goes with you. It's very selfish, but it's understandable."
- Mick Jagger

Once upon a time there was a boy named Clovus who lived in a beautiful forest of fir trees with three bears. The bears were his only family and he loved them. Clovus could remember nothing of his life prior to the three bears. Yet, in his heart Clovus knew that he didn't quite belong. Something was very different about him. He tried to climb the trees in the forest to retrieve honey, but he always fell, raking his knees down the rough bark during his descent. This was increasingly disheartening for young Clovus. It also caused him to examine himself more closely and more frequently.

He noticed that he didn't have fur like the other bears. He didn't have claws like them either. He couldn't run as fast as they could. In fact, he didn't even know his name *was* Clovus, for he couldn't speak the language of men. Clovus was forced to grunt and growl like the three bears, which caused considerable frustration and miscommunication. Poor Clovus often confused the grunting one should make for *hunger* with the grunting one should make for *wrestle,* for they sounded very similar. Consequently, these frequent mistakes left him mildly brain damaged and temporarily crippled. Still, Clovus hated to brag, but he felt somehow smarter and more intelligent than his three furry friends.

One day something magical happened. A visitor ventured to the forest. He was a human creature just like Clovus and his name was Regigus. Regigus, with his keen eye, discovered Clovus in the thick of the wood and before Clovus or the bears knew what had happened, the boy was sitting down in the most-luxurious house you ever saw freshly bathed and clothed like royalty—for such he was. Regigus had found his long lost son who went missing from birth when the housemaid mistakenly threw out the slumbering Clovus with the soiled household linens.

As time passed, Clovus learned to speak and formulate thoughts. And more importantly, he discovered who he really was. Yet to this day, on nights when the weather is nice, Clovus will sneak off into the wood, crawl on all fours, scratch his back against the trees and grunt and growl until the piercing morning sunrise brings warmth to the earth and brings Clovus back to his senses.

The Pendulum Swing

Believe it or not, there are some distinct similarities between poor Clovus and us. You see, I think most of us live a great deal of our lives somewhere on the path between faith and doubt. Much like Clovus, we live in this back-and-forth cycle between being a human and being a bear—between faith and doubt. Deep down, we know we're human, but constantly we find ourselves drawn back to life

The Discovery: Beyond the Jesus of Flapjacks and Grilled Cheese

as a bear. We know that a life of faith is characteristic of a Christ-follower, but the life of doubt constantly calls to us, appealing to us. We are caught in this pendulum swing between faith and doubt. Doubt and faith. Back and forth. Believing things, but never quite sure what. This is a well-trodden path that meanders back and forth between the two trails of faith and doubt, and many are its travelers.

This path for me takes on various forms. For example, my faith says that the Carolina Panthers will make a comeback in the middle of their losing streak to win the NFC championship and go on to the Super Bowl. But my doubt says more convincingly that it won't happen. My faith says that this will be the year that the Rolling Stones realize that their dynasty ended decades ago and will finally let go of their insatiable desire to wear tight leather pants and stumble around a stage looking like they just escaped from a nursing home. But my doubt says that these geriatric juggernauts of rock 'n' roll won't be giving it up anytime soon.

But this path also leads me down more serious and life-altering trails as well. Sometimes my faith says that America is on the cusp of another spiritual awakening where we will see hundreds of thousands, if not millions of men and women, high school and college students, boys and girls, grandmas and grandpas enter into a life-changing relationship with Jesus Christ, so much so that it changes the very landscape and makeup of American culture. On the other hand, my doubt often screams louder in my ear saying that no such revival will ever take place in America again. We are too far gone. The next step will be for God to eradicate us off the map like He did with Sodom and Gomorrah (Genesis 19) because of their heinous sin against a holy God. Sometimes my faith says that God can take my life and use me like He used the Apostle Paul to reach the entire known world of his day with the Gospel of Christ. But my doubt says that I've got too much baggage in my past and too much junk in my life for God to ever be able to use me in that capacity.

If I haven't missed the mark here, I think I'm right in assuming that most of us as followers of Christ at various times in our lives live in this pendulum swing. And it's not as if it's some kind of new phenomenon. As we dive into John 11, we'll discover that one of Jesus' good friends traveled the very same winding path.

Martha's Winding Path

The first verse of chapter eleven explains that Jesus' friend Lazarus was sick. We don't find out how bad off he really was until we read verse eleven. Without anyone bringing Him the news, Jesus knew that Lazarus had died (maybe because He's God!).

Now, fast forward four days later. Jesus finally arrived with His entourage at the home of Lazarus and his two sisters, Mary and Martha. Martha was the first to speak to Jesus and, like most of us would have done, she questioned Him about His impeccable timing:

"Lord, *if* You had been here, my brother wouldn't have died. *Yet* even now I know that whatever You ask from God, God will give You" (John 11:21-22).

Such is the way the conversation began between Jesus and Martha. She offered no traditional greeting of "Shalom!" There was no "Hey Jesus, I'm glad You finally made it!" No "Jesus, can I get You something to drink from our goat?" Nothing like that. It was straight to the point for Martha. In the midst of her doubt and pain she did the only thing she knew to do, lay the guilt of Lazarus' death on Jesus, the One who *could* have healed him had He been there. However, in the midst of her doubt, she mustered up what little faith she had left adding, "Yet even now I know that whatever You ask from God, God will give You." Somehow in this winding path between faith and doubt, she blamed Jesus on one hand, yet on the other she believed that Jesus could still do *something*, though she wasn't sure what.

Jesus then told Martha that Lazarus would rise again, but Martha's confusion about what Jesus meant demanded more explanation:

"Jesus said to her, 'I am the resurrection and the life. The one who believes in Me, even if he dies, will live. Everyone who believes in Me will never die—ever. Do you believe this?' 'Yes, Lord,' she told Him, 'I believe You are the Messiah, the Son of God, who was to come into the world'" (John 11:25-27).

This is the seventh *I AM* statement in John. And it's one that is packed full of truth. He said, "I AM the Resurrection and the Life." The word *resurrection* here literally means "to stand up again" pointing to a future a moment where Christ Himself would be raised from the dead. But more than that, Jesus was drawing a link between life and faith.[1] He was bringing her to a crisis point of decision where she must decide whether she could consciously put her faith in Jesus, the One from whom all life flows. Her response is beautiful. "I believe You are the Messiah, the Son of God." This is the strongest way she could have testified to Jesus' deity and authority. The word *believe* is in the perfect tense, meaning, "I have believed in the past, I believe now and I will continue believing into the future, whatever the future holds!" This is an incredible statement revealing that Martha was back on the path of faith. But she soon wandered over into doubt again, as we all do:

"'Remove the stone,' Jesus said. Martha, the dead man's sister, told Him, 'Lord, *he already stinks*. It's been four days'" (John 11:39).

As if Jesus had forgotten the crucial detail that Lazarus' body was already beginning to decompose, Martha interrupted Him. Standing there in her doubt, Martha tried to put the breaks on the whole resurrection process. Unsure of what Jesus was planning to do or was capable of doing, she followed the path back toward the land of doubt. And what I love about this whole conversation is Jesus' continued patience with Martha—patience completely characteristic of the real Jesus.

"Jesus said to her, 'Didn't I tell you that if you believed you would see the glory of God'" (John 11:40)?

And then, not a moment too soon, Jesus prayed to His Father and then immediately called the reeking, putrid Lazarus out of the tomb—the seventh sign in John. His patience was displayed with Martha. His power was displayed in Lazarus. His purpose was displayed to the entire crowd.

"… so they may believe You sent Me" (John 11:42).

The reality is, the wrestling match between faith and doubt that we see with Martha is the same wrestling match we all face. The question is, do we trust Jesus or not? If He calls you to a third world country to pastor a church, do you believe that He will give you what it takes to do it? If He is tugging on your heart to witness to your friend in Western Civ, will you take that step of faith believing that He will give you the words to say? If He is calling you to give a large percentage of your income to your church's building fund, will you do it believing that He owns it all anyway?

What I've discovered on this journey between faith and doubt is that there are never times when I don't need God's grace prevailing in my life, regardless of how good or bad a day I think I've had in the area of my faith performance. Jerry Bridges, one of my favorite writers, put it this way:

> Your worst days are never so bad that you are beyond the reach of God's grace. And your best days are never so good that you are beyond the need of God's grace.[2]

Thank you, Lord, for your continued patience with us and grace toward us in the midst of our journey between faith and doubt.

Feeding Your Appetite

When you find yourself veering down the path of doubt, what are some ways that you can determine in your heart to say as Martha did, "I believe You, Lord!" and then to act consistently that way?

What types of circumstances or feelings usually cause you to veer down the path of doubt?

What doubts are you currently facing or have recently resolved regarding God, His promises, Scripture, or just life in general?

How has God acted patiently toward you recently? Thank Him for that patience.

Your Discovery

12

Where Feet and Hair Collide
John 12

"I'm a big woman. I need big hair."
- Aretha Franklin

One of my favorite accounts in the whole New Testament happens right here in John 12—when Mary anointed Jesus' feet with her hair—one of the most humbling acts of service a person could ever provide in that culture. What I love most about this passage is the insight it provides into worship.

Worship is my heartbeat. I love to see God's people come together to lift high the name of Jesus without reservation. Whether I'm writing a new worship song or simply choosing songs for a worship set, my goal is that they be rich in biblical truth—deep enough to allow biblical scholars to worship freely, and yet simple enough that a new follower of Jesus can understand what's being sung and experience that same sense of intimacy with Christ. There's a balance there that I'm still learning. But it's a balance that Mary found strikingly simple. Her act of worship was deep and profound as she honored Him with the oil fit for a king; yet, it was amazingly simple because all she knew to do was to bow before Him and scrub His dirty feet. That's worship—profound and simple at the same time. Mary's example gives us some great insight into genuine, biblical worship.

1. She worshiped willfully.

Notice all of the action verbs involved in Mary's worship:

"Then Mary *took* a pound of fragrant oil—pure and expensive nard—*anointed* Jesus' feet, and *wiped* His feet with her hair" (John 12:3).

In just one verse, John emphasized her willful act of worship through careful detail. It was this type of specific and willful action that brought her close to the heart of the Savior.

Worship is not something that passively happens to you.
Worship is something that happens in you.

Worship is something you are actively involved *in*. Worship is a conscious choice. Many Christ-followers miss the point. I can't begin to count how many times I've heard someone say this in response to a Sunday worship service: "The worship was awesome today. The band was really on their game." Or, "Well, the worship wasn't all that great today. Billy Bob missed a few chord changes." I've said it too. But no matter how incredible or how terrible the music might have been, to make statements like these misses the point. Worship is not the songs we sing or the tune to which we sing them. Don't hear me say that music is not important. I definitely believe that worship *can* happen through song. And certainly the music we make should be done with excellence and quality.

But worship is more than that. It involves the willful action and obedience of the entire being—not just the lips. There is no more beautiful a harmony to the ears of God than a mouth expressing His greatness and a life expressing the same through its actions. Did you catch that?

> *Worship is a conscious choice of bringing our confession and our actions into harmony.*

We confess the holiness and awesomeness of God. And then we act on it. It's all about Jesus and our active participation in telling Him just how great He is. Worship is not about our preferences and not about what may or may not have sounded good at church.

2. She worshiped unashamedly.

Verse three says that after Mary anointed Jesus' feet, "the house was filled with *the fragrance* of the oil."

We shouldn't miss the importance of this little phrase. To say that the house "was filled with the fragrance of the oil" means that anyone and everyone in the house or within smell-shot of the house would have smelled the sweet aroma. There was no mistaking what Mary had done. And she didn't care who knew. She was unashamed to tell the whole neighborhood that Jesus was the object of her worship. And it was obvious to everyone.

My son is still too young to care about pooping in his pants. He loves it. He flaunts his stench around the house and out in public with no shame. If the President of the United States were visiting our home, Zeke would run up to him unabashedly and unhindered complete with runny nose and stinky diaper.

I wish some of those innocent, unashamed, childlike characteristics would remain through adulthood. Not that we would all wear adult diapers, but that we would live unashamed lives, especially in our worship of Jesus—that we would flaunt our love for Christ with little concern for who finds out—that we would desire for the world to smell the aroma of our love for Christ.

Here's how the apostle Paul described the aroma that we have as believers in Christ:

"For to God we are the fragrance of Christ among those who are being saved and among those who are perishing" (2 Corinthians 2:15).

To a world that is lost and dying, we are the fragrance of Christ. We flaunt the scent of Christ to a lost world. Mary understood this. And she did it unashamedly.

3. She worshiped humbly.

For some reason whenever I think of dirty, grimy, nasty feet, my mind always pulls up a mental picture stashed away from watching *The Lord of the Rings*. Remember Frodo's hairy feet? Why that comes to mind? I'm not sure. I don't imagine that Jesus' feet were quite that hairy, but they were no doubt just as dirty and nasty. Sandals were the shoes of choice. Dirt was the highway of choice—the *only* highway, actually. On the dusty paths of Israeli terrain, no feet could have gone far without being totally covered and consumed with dust, grime, mire and filth.

Now contrast the disgusting feet of a middle-eastern man with the elaborate, beautiful hair of a middle-eastern woman. In that culture the hair of a woman was her most prized possession. It was considered her beauty covering and her glory (1 Corinthians 11:15). Her hair was connected to her essence—what others thought of her and who she considered herself to be. And yet in spite of the cultural importance of her hair, Mary used her beauty covering in the same way she would have used a dirty washcloth. Picture the beautiful, immaculate, long flowing hair of Mary scrubbing the filth, mud and grime off of the feet of the Savior. To say this was a humbling act is an understatement. This was a *humiliating* act. This was a degrading act. This was an act of total self-abandonment. She threw caution to the wind. She humbled herself by giving up the one thing that gave her honor and dignity, and she sacrificed it for a few moments to worship at the feet of Jesus.

Genuine worship is about coming to the feet of Jesus in total humility. It's about abandoning what we are driven to hold on to—what we think brings us dignity and honor. It's about saying, "God, the world says I need to drive a Hummer and live in a massive house by the back nine and go to my beach house on the weekends, BUT You have called me to take food, medicine and the Gospel to the slum children in Johannesburg, South Africa, so that's what I'll do." Or, "God, the world says _____, BUT You have told me to _____." You fill in the blanks. I don't know where the rubber meets the road for you. If we are honest, most of us are living safe in the four walls of our preppy middle-class school or work environment and no one knows that we secretly follow Christ. But what would happen if people knew?

God forbid!

What sacrifice would it mean? True worship means that we count all as loss for the sake of knowing Christ.

> "More than that, I also consider everything to be *a loss* in view of *the surpassing value of knowing Christ* Jesus my Lord. Because of Him I have suffered the loss of all things and consider them filth, so that I may gain Christ" (Philippians 3:8).

4. She worshiped unreservedly.

What about the perfume? Why was it significant? From Judas' stupid remark in verse five, we discover that it is worth 300 denarii, which lands somewhere in the neighborhood of one year's wages or about ten thousand dollars.[1] Many scholars believe that Mary could have been saving this for her dowry—the costly gift that she would one day bring into her marriage. Instead, she poured it out at the feet of Jesus unreservedly. She kept nothing back. It was expensive. It was costly. It was important to her. Yet she gave it all. She anointed Jesus' feet with the same oil that was to be reserved and held for the most important person in her life. And she worshiped Jesus, not as her husband, but as her Lord and Savior—not as a mere human being, but as the God of the universe. One commentator described worship this way:

> In praising a creature, we may easily exceed the truth; but in praising God we have only to go on confessing what
> He really is to us.[2]

That's what Mary did. And if she could have, she probably would have sat at His feet forever. She gave all that was important to her. And she gave it without reservation or hesitation.

Mary teaches us what genuine worship is all about.

It's willful. It's a conscious, active choice—a choice that supercedes feelings and opinions.

It's bold. There's no shame in true worship. It tells the world of our love for and devotion to Christ.

It's wrought in humility. There is no place for ego in the worship of God. It's abandoning our will in submission to God's.

And it's unreserved. It's costly. It's expensive.

Worship involves giving to God what matters most to us and what He desires most from us.

Feeding Your Appetite

How does your current thinking about worship conflict or agree with true biblical worship?

Josh defined worship as "a conscious choice of bringing our confession and our actions into harmony." Do you agree or disagree? Why or why not?

How would you rate the aroma of Christ in your life? Do the people around you easily smell the sweet fragrance of Christ, or do they have to sniff pretty hard to catch a whiff?

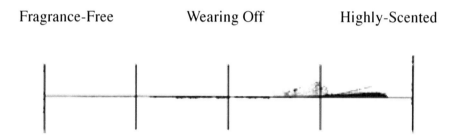

Fragrance-Free   Wearing Off   Highly-Scented

Based on John 12, come up with your own definition of worship

Your Discovery

13

Reinstate Slavery
John 13

"Nothing sets a person so out of the devil's reach as humility."
- Jonathan Edwards

The year was 1996. The month was March. The number one rock song of the ARC Weekly Top 40 was "One of Us" performed by Joan Osborne.[1] The song spoke honestly and vulnerably about what the world might be like if God were one of us—if God stooped down from heaven to become one of us. To live where we live. To experience what we experience. Osborne whined out the chorus:

> What if God was one of us,
> Just a slob like one of us,
> Just a stranger on the bus,
> Trying to make his way home?[2]

The song poses soul-searching questions to the listener—questions about what you might call God to His face and what you might ask Him if you could only ask Him one question. The song was an attempt to air publicly the questions that we all ask privately—the question of whether God is relatable—the question of whether or not God did, at some point, become one of us—the truth we all seek.

Osborne's hit song has since been classified as a "one hit wonder." But in spite of its short reign, it grabbed the attention of music lovers and truth seekers around the world. Questions were raised. People began putting themselves in the song. And those types of questions are still being asked today.

Did God become one of us? Joan Osborne left us still needing answers. John the Apostle answered with an emphatic,

"YES! HE DID BECOME ONE OF US!"

In fact, He didn't just become one of us; He became our *servant*. He became our foot-washing *slave*. This was exactly John's point for including chapter thirteen. And he was careful to describe the scene in great detail.

> "So He got up from supper, laid aside His robe, took a towel, and tied it around Himself. Next, He poured water into a basin and began to wash His disciples' feet and to dry them with the towel tied around Him" (John 13:4-5).

Sure, we all know this was an act of humility. Even in our own culture where foot washing is often labeled as weird, out-of-the-ordinary and reserved for the snake-kissing, poison-drinking, mountain cults, it is also viewed as a sincere act of service from one to another. But in Jewish culture, even more so. Foot washing was an act of absolute humility, as we've already seen from Mary's example in chapter twelve. In Jewish culture, before a meal such as this, it was customary for a slave or servant boy to wash the feet of every guest. In this case, the disciples' feet should have already been washed.

We can't see behind the scenes, but I can just imagine Jesus kindly dismissing the servant boy from his duties and taking the bowl and the towel from him. As Jesus walks over to the disciples and begins washing their feet, I can imagine the servant boy keeling over from shock at what he's seeing. Under no circumstances was something like this to take place. This was the job of the slave. This was the job of the lowliest of servants. Yet, Jesus did it. Jesus performed the act. Jesus took it upon Himself to wash the disgusting, calloused, rugged feet of His disciples.

If you're like me, you may not like for people to serve you or wait on you hand and foot. Especially when it involves a significant amount of sacrifice on the part of the server. I start feeling uncomfortable and lazy. On a recent mission trip to South Korea, I battled these feelings almost constantly. The Korean people waited on me like I was a celebrity. They served me endlessly. And it bothered me. It was a major adjustment. But that's Korean culture and it was totally foreign to me.

This is probably how Peter felt. He knew that what Jesus was doing was slave work. No wonder he reacted the way he did. No wonder he raised his voice at Jesus screaming,

"You will never wash my feet—ever" (John 14:3)!

"The master of the universe, washing my feet? That's absurd," Peter must have thought. But Peter failed to understand the significance. And so Jesus persisted because Peter had to be taught the way of the servant—that he must be the last of all and the servant of all (Mark 9:35)—that the last will be first and the first will be last (Matthew 20:16).

It should have needed no explanation, but Jesus wanted to make sure His guys got the point. He told them,

"So if I, your Lord and Teacher, have washed your feet, you also ought to wash one another's feet. For I have given you an example that you also should do just as I have done for you" (John 13:14-15).

I can imagine the disciples still sitting there dumbfounded at what had just happened. But for a few of them, maybe the light came on. Maybe it registered. Maybe they realized that this was their example to follow—that they were servants too.

Replacing What's Been Lost

I'm convinced that servanthood is a concept that has been lost in much of the Christian community today. Or at the very least misunderstood. It's been replaced with the modern psychological method—the "let's chant 'I believe in myself' while we quickly flip the channel past the swollen-bellied, flies-in-the-face African kids" mentality—the "God wants to bless you with a new BMW if you give to my ministry" kind of flapjack Christianity that stands in direct contradistinction to what Jesus just demonstrated in this passage. From the televangelists to the top-selling inspirational authors of our nation, the whimsical, magical message of the genie-in-the-bottle, wish-granting God has led astray people all over the world resulting in grilled cheese worship and a misunderstanding of servanthood—one of the major concepts of the Christian faith. And service was Jesus' heartbeat. That's why He came. That's why He left the glory of heaven. That's why He took on sinful human flesh. Paul put it best in Philippians:

> "who, existing in the form of God, did not consider equality with God as something to be used for His own advantage. Instead He emptied Himself by assuming the form of a slave, taking on the likeness of men ..." (Philippians 2:6-7a).

Jesus came assuming the form of a slave, not a master. He took the form of a slave, not a conquering king. He took the form of a slave, not a gladiator competing for the praise and sympathy of the masses. He never told the disciples to expect fame and glory from following Him. Not at all. He told them the direct opposite. He told them to expect persecution, heartache, and ultimately death. He told them,

> "whoever wants to be first among you must be your slave; just as the Son of Man did not come to be served, but to serve, and to give His life—a ransom for many" (Matthew 20:27-28).

The Discovery: Beyond the Jesus of Flapjacks and Grilled Cheese

Jesus came to serve. His service led to His death. His death was our ransom. And His call still goes out. He asks, "Do you want to follow Me? Then you must serve. Do you want to follow Me? Then you must humble yourself, kneel down and scrub feet." That's the heart of a servant. That's what weeds out the pansies. And that's what separates genuine Christ-followers from the rest of the crowd.

Now, e-mail Joan Osborne and tell her what you discovered from John 13.

Feeding Your Appetite

In what ways does the concept of biblical servanthood conflict with the culture in which we live?

In what ways does biblical servanthood stand in contrast to what many TV preachers claim?

Read Philippians 2:5-11 and thank Jesus for humbling Himself like He did to scrub your guilty feet.

Your Discovery

14

Directionally Challenged
John 14

> "What can you say about a society that says God is dead
> and Elvis is alive?"
> - Irv Kupcinet

No book is complete without a story involving a husband and wife lost in the car together. Every couple has at least one such story. For Tasha and me, it happened not so long ago. It was around 6 pm and we were driving home with two starving kids in the backseat. With only a few miles left to go, I threw a clever smirk on my face like I had just discovered drinking water in a barren desert. With an excited, adventurous-looking glimmer in my eye, I convinced Tasha that I knew a short-cut home in order to miss the annoying gridlock traffic. An hour later, after ignoring my wife's countless pleas to pull over and ask for directions, we finally pulled into our driveway.

The kids? Quiet and comatose in the back from malnutrition.

Tasha? Hair lying on the floorboard at her feet, blood squirting from her patchy scalp from pulling out handfuls of hair in shear frustration.

Me? Hands held high basking in the victory of my accomplishment as an EMS crew initiated IV drips for Tasha and the kids.

To this day I'm not sure how we made it home. I'm pretty sure an angel pitched in some help after having a good sidesplitting laugh and finally feeling sorry for the poor sap at the wheel. Needless to say, we now have a navigation system. And sometimes I hit the *detour* button just for fun to get a reaction out of Tasha. Not amused, she immediately switches it back to *normal* mode.

Directions. We all need them to get where we're going. Some of us ignore them more than others (sorry Tasha), but we all have to have them. I think it's human nature to want to know where we are and how to get where we're going—not only in a physical sense, but also in a spiritual sense. In John 14, we discover the disciples revolting against the male tendency to *not* ask directions. Instead, they wanted Jesus to map out every detail for them. So, they asked questions—questions about Jesus—about God the Father—about how to get to God. These are questions that we've all asked. Whether we've put them in concrete terms matters not. The human soul begs for the answers—answers that John sought to expose through specific accounts of Jesus' life.

John 14 begins what scholars call the *Farewell Discourse*. It begins Jesus' lengthy speech to His disciples just before He went to the cross—a speech revealing more of His identity, the identity of Christ-followers, and what our purpose is on this earth.

Jesus began by telling the disciples His plan—a plan that shouldn't have required any further instructions or directions. But nevertheless, they needed them, just like we do. Jesus said,

> "'I am going away to prepare a place for you ... You know the way where I am going.' 'Lord,' Thomas said, 'we don't know where You're going. How can we know the way'" (John 14:2, 4-5)?

Thomas, oblivious to Jesus' intent, sought literal directions. What Jesus said next is a fundamental verse of the Christian faith and separates Him from every other religious teacher who ever walked the planet:

"Jesus told him, 'I am *the way, the truth,* and *the life*. No one comes to the Father except through Me'" (John 14:6).

The Way

Let's break down these three words, *way, truth* and *life* and dig a little deeper. Some would say that Jesus' statement is too exclusive. My response is, "Yes. That's the point." Jesus was saying, "Look guys, I'm not just one way among many ways to the Father. I'm the *only* way." If you think about it, it only makes sense. If you asked me directions to my house, I wouldn't say, "Ahhh, just pick an interstate and drive until you feel like turning off" (Unless maybe I didn't like you that much)! That would be insane! What's insane is that people choose this method when it comes to their eternal destiny—the flip of the coin method—the fix-your-baked-potato-how-you-like-it method. But it doesn't work that way. Jesus said matter-of-factly, "I am the way!" Christ echoed this same idea earlier in John 10 when He said,

"I am the door. If anyone enters by Me, he will be saved and will come in and go out and find pasture" (John 10:9)

The door to the Father is one—not many. The door of salvation is one—not many. This is echoed all throughout Scripture. The Lord said in Isaiah,

"No god was formed before Me, and there will be none after Me. I, I am the Lord, and there is no other Savior but Me" (Isaiah 43:10-11).

Josh McDowell was lecturing at a university when a student posed the question, "Evidently you have proven that Jesus Christ is the Son of God. (But) aren't there other ways also to a relationship with God?"[1] Here was Josh's response:

> I answered the student by saying that many people don't understand the nature of God. Usually the question is, "How can a loving God allow a sinful individual to go to Hell?" I would ask, "How can a holy, just, righteous God allow a sinful individual into His presence?"[2]

The student asked the wrong question. And this is where people confuse the issue. They think that God is *obligated* to let them into heaven because He's a loving God. The problem is, they forget that He's also just—that He's obligated to punish sin. That's why Christ died—to take our punishment on Himself (1 Peter 2:24). And that's why He alone is the door, the only way of salvation.

The Truth

The other night Tasha and I were flipping through the television channels when we came across a behind the scenes look at Fox's top-rated *Prison Break*. In an interview with Wentworth Miller, the main character who plays Michael Scofield, the interviewer asked the question, "What do you like most about acting?" His response was enlightening to say the least. He said that since he grew up in a home that was pretty "straight-laced" he enjoyed the opportunity that acting brings along to "act inappropriately." In other words, he felt free to do whatever he wanted in front of a camera and not be held accountable for it.

If this attitude doesn't describe the mentality of American culture, I don't know what does. It's the in-front-of-a-camera mentality that I can do whatever I want and feel no remorse or sense of accountability for my actions.

We live in a culture of decay—a culture where truth is relative—a culture of no absolutes—a culture that invites us all to do whatever we want and feel no remorse—a culture that "has dispensed with Truth and has replaced it with truths."[3] But Jesus came declaring,

"I *am* the Truth. There *are* absolutes. There *is* a standard. And that standard is *Me*."

The reality is though, even followers of Christ, redeemed sons and daughters of the King of Kings, struggle with the issue of truth. Joel Belz of *World* magazine said,

> There is a perverse assumption now ... dominant among evangelicals (Bible-believing, Christ-followers) that feelings, attitudes, and relationships are all more important than truth.[4]

I think this assumption is most evident in social and ethical issues. So we ask questions like, "Is it okay to abort my baby if I was raped? Can I lie to protect a person's reputation? What are the sexual limits for my girlfriend and me? Is God a Republican? Can I steal a road sign to hang in my room? Would Jesus recycle? Can I murder my neighbor's cat if it sheds in my yard?" (Okay, some of these are intentionally ridiculous for the sake of provoking you to a quick laugh so you'll be more susceptible to the truth when it slaps you in the face). But if we are honest with ourselves, at the heart of many of the questions we ask is a hint of hypocrisy. We want to know how close we can get to the fire without getting burned. Instead our attitude should be, "How far away from the fire can I stay?" But I don't want to shrug off honest questions either. It is true that there are many gray issues that the Bible simply doesn't address. That's why Jesus didn't stop there. Later in John 14 He gave at least two criteria to determine truth. He said,

> "If you love Me, you will keep My commandments. And I will ask the Father, and He will give you another Counselor to be with you forever. He is the Spirit of truth" (John 14:15-17a).

Here they are:

1. Obey Scripture – "Keep my commandments."

If Scripture is clear on an issue, that's the bottom line. We don't need to sit around and debate whether homosexuality is right or wrong. Scripture is clear that it is sin (Leviticus 20:13, Romans 1:27, Genesis 19). We don't have to argue about sex outside of marriage. Scripture is clear that it is sin (Deuteronomy 22:22, 1 Thessalonians 4:3, Proverbs 5:15, 7:6-27, Matthew 1:18-19). Where the Bible is clear, we must also be clear.

2. Obey the Holy Spirit – "He is the Spirit of truth."

But what about the gray issues I mentioned earlier? What do we do with those? Smoking? Moderate alcohol use? Stuff like that? The Holy Spirit is the key. The Spirit living inside of us is our truth barometer, our measurement for determining truth. When something isn't clearly spelled out in Scripture, the person of the Holy Spirit guides us into all truth (John 16:13). He convicts us of sin (John 16:8). He speaks for us (Matthew 10:19, Romans 8:26). He gives us assurance that we are God's children (Romans 8:16). He comforts us in affliction (2 Corinthians 1:4).

What one Christ-follower may have a strong conviction against, another may feel the freedom to participate in. Social drinking is one of these issues, particularly in the South. Let me let you in on something that has helped me in trying to figure out where I stand on many of these gray issues. If I'm not sure about something, I ask myself this question,

"Will my participation in this activity cause another Christ-follower to get the wrong idea and possibly stumble into sin, or worse, will it cause an unbeliever to be totally turned off to Christianity?"

If I can't answer this with an affirmative *No*, I steer away from it because I'd rather err on the side of caution.

The Life

There's a song by Charlie Hall that repeats the beautiful refrain, "life flows from God, it flows from God." Every time I hear it I'm reminded of that fact—that God is the source of all life—that wherever His river flows, life springs up (Ezekiel 47:9)—that the "Spirit is the One who gives life" (John 6:63)—that everlasting life is His desire for all men (2 Peter 3:9). If He is the way (which He is) and if He is the truth (which He is), it only follows logically that He is the life. You and I cannot have everlasting, abundant, purposeful, clearly directed life apart from entering through the door, the Way, Jesus Christ. And you and I cannot live meaningful, culture-changing, Christ-exalting, truth-exposing lives apart from living and abiding in the source of all truth, the Spirit of Truth, Jesus Himself, as He leads and guides us into all truth.

Feeding Your Appetite

What response would you give to someone who says that followers of Christ are narrow-minded, intolerant, and exclusive in regards to other religious systems?

What gray issues have you struggled with in your own heart in trying to discern right and wrong? What influenced your decision?

The Discovery: Beyond the Jesus of Flapjacks and Grilled Cheese

What are some standards in your personal or social life that you may need to re-evaluate so that you err on the side of caution?

If you have some extra time, study what Paul says in 1 Corinthians 10:23-33 about Christian liberty.

Your Discovery

15

Obsessed with Foliage
John 15

"The last time I saw him he was walking down lover's lane holding his own hand."
- Fred Allen

Some people have an unhealthy obsession with plants. Growing up in the 80s, I remember thinking my mom was one of these people. At the time, it was popular to beautify one's home with multiple hanging potted plants. At least, it was popular in our home. Surrounding and cradling each plant, a neatly woven wicker basket swung, complete with a shellac finish and usually adorned with some sort of wooden farm animal. This was my mom's kitchen. Her haven. She loved plants. Still does. I often wondered if this was normal.

God definitely has a sense of humor; because now I'm married to a woman who has a very similar love for and obsession with plants. This type of love is foreign to me. A love for pizza? Absolutely! A love for loud music, video games, and fast cars? Totally! But plants? No. Plants have a very tiny place and hold very little value in this heart of mine. Don't get me wrong. I'm grateful that God made them, because I suppose we need them. But there's certainly no compulsive drive within me to adorn my living environment with an endless amount of plant life and vegetation. I have friends whose offices look like the Amazon rainforest. I once lost my son in a 12' by 8' room thickly adorned with a seemingly endless array of ficus trees and various plastic plants. I wanted to ask my friend what joy he received out of this. I held my tongue instead and just searched for my missing son.

Had my mom and wife lived during Jesus' time, they would have been captivated by His use of one particular metaphor above all the rest. You guessed it. Plants. Jesus often used plants to teach lessons to His disciples. John 15 is one example. This chapter reminds us of the importance of staying connected to Christ as the life-giving source. The key verse of the chapter makes this clear.

> "I am *the vine*; you are *the branches*. The one who remains in Me and I in him produces much fruit, because you can do nothing without Me" (John 15:5).

I can easily imagine Jesus and His disciples walking through a garden or courtyard adorned with hanging vines and vegetation that would have acted as natural visual aids. What the disciples had yet to realize was that they were about to be physically separated from Jesus in a way they never imagined. Jesus was only hours away from being crucified on a Roman cross, and yet in light of His impending death, He taught His disciples the importance of connection to Him, the true vine—connection to the source of life.

The word *remain* is one of the key words for the book of John, and it appears eleven times in this chapter. Some translations use the word *abide* which is also a good translation. The word implies an active connectedness to the life-source.

Dogs and Ego

My siblings and I owned about thirty dogs during our childhoods—one dog at a time. We couldn't keep them alive. I think we were cursed. You've heard of having a brown thumb because you can't keep plants alive? Well, this was brown thumb of the K-9 sort. I once was riding my school bus when it ran over my cocker spaniel, Brandy. Cursed I tell you! I was cursed! For a ten-year-old kid, watching your bleeding, dying dog take his last breath and feeling like an accomplice in the act does wonders for your self-esteem. Since we struggled simply to keep our dogs alive, training them to obey commands was not even on our radar. Keeping breath in their lungs was our main priority.

Nonetheless, every now and then my brothers and I would experiment with a few simple commands like "STAY!" I'm convinced our dogs thought we were yelling "STEAK!" because they turned on the speed like Jessica Simpson turns on a hair dryer. There was no staying involved. No staying would be done that day or any other day. But every now and then, when the stars aligned, we could bribe our dogs with a treat just long enough to get them to sit and stay for a few seconds. It was a glorious moment—one for the scrapbook. But what I realized was that my dogs' temporary obedience was not out of love for their masters but out of sheer dogged (excuse the pun) selfishness. They wanted the reward. Nothing more.

The remaining that Jesus is talking about is the direct opposite. This is a remaining that happens out of love for the Master. It's ongoing. It's willing obedience. It doesn't seek a reward. It's not selfish. It's a type of remaining that happens when the disciple has lost all sense of ego and pride—all sense of *me*-driven agenda—all sense of the I-can-do-this-on-my-own mentality.

The moment that the branch becomes disconnected from the vine, the main arteries of life-giving power are shut off and eliminated.

I cannot even begin to count how many times I've talked to teenagers or individuals who have disconnected from God. They come to me all the time saying, "Josh, I don't know what's happening. I'm slipping into sin. I've started partying again ... bla bla bla."

What's happening? I'll tell you what's happening. The branch disconnected from the vine! Somewhere along the way, the branch decided that it would be fine apart from its life source. Maybe they stopped having a daily, intimate time of Bible study and prayer. Maybe they stopped having fellowship with other Christ-followers on a regular basis. Maybe they stopped sharing their faith with their friends. Maybe they continually ignored God's voice and the Spirit's promptings in their life. Or maybe they performed all the right actions, but they did so out of a sense of obligation. Or maybe they, like my occasionally obedient dog, just wanted the reward. Whatever the case, *abiding* and *remaining* involve a faith-connection to the vine. Abiding means I don't say, "Look how awesome I am for staying connected to the vine!" Abiding means I *do* say, "Wow, look how awesome the vine is for pumping into me the source of life!" That's the difference. The branch has no place for ego.

"... because you can do nothing without Me"

Ego has no place in the work of God. Pride and ego are in direct opposition to the life that flows from the vine to the branches. Ernest Legouvé, the French dramatist, said,

> If he could only see how small a vacancy his death would leave, the proud man would think less of the place he occupies in his lifetime.[1]

He's right. How easy it is to begin to think that it's all about us—that it's our own power that keeps us connected to the vine—that whatever accomplishments or place we occupy on earth is somehow because of something *we* do—that we carry significance apart from the vine. But nothing could be further from the truth.

Staying Connected

Here's an honest question that you might be thinking—"How do I know if I'm staying attached to the vine? How do I know if I've somehow *de*tached myself?" Great question! Isaiah has some answers for us. In Isaiah chapter five, God described Israel as a beautiful vineyard—a vineyard that He lovingly created to bear luscious, beautiful, delicious fruit—fruit that would bear witness to Him as the Savior for all nations. Instead, Isaiah says that the vineyard produced "worthless grapes" (Isaiah 5:2)—completely foul and detestable. Israel became disconnected from the source of life and therefore produced rotten fruit, useful for nothing. That's why Jesus said,

> "The one who remains in Me and I in him produces much fruit ..."

That's it! Fruit! Fruit is the evidence. Have you examined your fruit lately? Because here's the clincher. A healthy branch produces healthy fruit. Healthy fruit is evidence of a healthy branch. And a healthy branch is evidence of a healthy connection to the vine. Galatians describes what some of this fruit looks like.

> "But the fruit of the Spirit is love, joy, peace, patience, kindness, goodness, faith, gentleness, self-control ..." (Galatians 5:22-23).

These are the fruits that bear witness to our connectedness to the vine. If I were to plant a fruit tree in my yard (as hard as it is for me to imagine), I would expect a specific type of fruit to grow depending on the type and health of the tree. Our fruit production as Christ-followers works the same way. If I am a healthy branch staying connected to the vine, I should produce the fruits I just mentioned.

In contrast, Galatians also gives us an idea of what rotten fruit looks like—the works of the flesh.

"Now the works of the flesh are obvious: sexual immorality, moral impurity, promiscuity, idolatry, sorcery, hatreds, strife, jealousy, outbursts of anger, selfish ambitions, dissensions, factions, envy, drunkenness, carousing, and anything similar ..." (Galatians 5:19-21).

When we detach ourselves from the vine, the works of the flesh begin to grow and worthless grapes begin to take over.

And what about this naughty list above? Aren't these rotten fruits true of only the really *bad* sinners? Actually, no. Because before we think we've got it all together, let's remember what Jesus said:

"But I tell you, everyone who looks at a woman to lust for her has already committed adultery with her in his heart" (Matthew 5:28).

Maybe you haven't physically committed sexual immorality, but Jesus said if you've done it in your heart, you're guilty. Bottom line? Fruit is connected to the heart.

Our connectedness to Christ determines the condition of our heart. And the condition of our heart determines the type of fruit we produce.

It's time for followers of Christ to begin obsessing over plant life—an obsession that is rooted (again, excuse the pun) in the true vine, Jesus Christ, our life-source.

Feeding Your Appetite

In what ways has self-centeredness and ego been a motivation in your walk with Christ?

Read Galatians 5:19-23 and make a list of the fruits of the Spirit that you think are most evident in your life. Which ones are lacking? Ask the Holy Spirit to help you develop the fruits that are the toughest for you to produce.

In examining the fruit from your own life, how would you rate your connectedness to Christ?

Securely Abiding   Sometimes Abiding   Never Abiding

|—————|—————|—————|—————|

Josh made the statement, "Our connectedness to Christ determines the condition of our heart. And the condition of our heart determines the type of fruit we produce." Try to think of an example in your own life of how all of this works together.

Your Discovery

16

A Time is Coming
John 16

"My dear Jesus, my Savior, is so deeply written on my heart, that I feel confident that if my heart were to be cut open and chopped to pieces, the name of Jesus would be found written on every piece."
- Ignatius, 111 AD – thrown to the lions in Rome

I have two goals for this chapter. First, I hope to open your eyes to a new or fresh awareness of the suffering of Christ-followers all around the world—suffering for the *cause* of Christ. Second, I hope to ignite in you a love for Christian biographies, especially biographies of Christ-followers who have paid the ultimate price for following Christ—suffering, persecution and sometimes death. Most of this chapter consists of excerpts from some of the books that have radically shaped my walk with Christ and my outlook on what it means to truly live a life that counts for the kingdom of God.

The Discovery: Beyond the Jesus of Flapjacks and Grilled Cheese

In preparing to write this, I again became overwhelmed with my own complacency as a follower of Christ living in my cozy, middle-class, suburban neighborhood, safe and oblivious from the atrocities that are going on all around the world. And that's my prayer for you as well.

In John 16, Jesus continued His farewell conversation with His disciples, reminding them that suffering is a part of following Christ. He told them,

> "They will ban you from the synagogues. In fact, *a time is coming* when anyone who kills you will think he is offering service to God. They will do these things because they haven't known the Father or Me" (John 16:2-3).

John didn't tell us what the disciples' reactions were, but I imagine they were not galloping and frolicking with joy. Disconcerted and confused are probably understatements. But Jesus, aware of what they were feeling, concluded with a word of hope and encouragement:

> "I have told you these things so that in Me you may have *peace*. In the world you have suffering ..." (John 16:33).

Right! Because news about torture, persecution and death always brings me peace!

If I was a disciple, at this point I'd be thinking, *"Okay Jesus, You've really lost it this time. A little too much bread and wine for ya, eh, big guy? Peace? Are you out of your mind? Peace? While I'm being beaten and flogged? Peace? While the oil is burning the skin off of my body? Peace? Wow, Jesus, You're a funny guy. Where's the hope in this, Jesus?"* But Jesus wasn't finished. The hope lies in the rest of verse thirty-three.

> "Be courageous! I have conquered the world."

Follow Jesus' logic.
A. *Suffering comes from the world.*
B. *I have overcome the world.*

C. Therefore, you have peace through Me in the midst of suffering.

The peace and courage Jesus provides comes in the middle of the suffering. It comes when the world is at odds with us. It comes at the most difficult times.

Richard Wurmbrand

Richard Wurmbrand was a Romanian Christian during the Communist reign. Outspoken for his faith in Christ and his feelings against atheistic Communism, Wurmbrand was eventually kidnapped and imprisoned for fourteen years. In *Tortured for Christ*, he recounted many of the atrocities that he saw and experienced. He wrote:

> Christians were hung upside-down on ropes and beaten so severely that their bodies swung back and forth under the blows. Christians were also placed in ice-box "refrigerator cells," which were so cold that frost and ice covered the inside. I was thrown into one while I had very little clothing on. Prison doctors would watch through an opening until they saw symptoms of freezing to death, then they would give a signal and guards would rush in to take us out and make us warm. When we were finally warmed, we would immediately be put back into the ice-box cells to freeze. Thawing out, then freezing to within minutes of death, then being thawed out—over and over again! Even today there are times when I can't bear to open a refrigerator.[1]

Many of Wurmbrand's friends and family were also tortured and executed for their faith in Christ. He recounted one such incident:

> A pastor by the name of Florescu was tortured with red-hot iron pokers and with knives. He was beaten very badly. Then starving rats were driven into his cell through a large

pipe. He could not sleep because he had to defend himself all the time. If he rested a moment, the rats would attack him.

He was forced to stand for two weeks, day and night. The Communists wished to compel him to betray his brethren, but he resisted steadfastly. Eventually, they brought his fourteen-year-old son to the prison and began to whip the boy in front of his father, saying that they would continue to beat him until the pastor said what they wished him to say. The poor man was half mad. He bore it as long as he could, then he cried to his son, "Alexander, I must say what they want! I can't bear your beating anymore!" The son answered, "Father, don't do me the injustice of having a traitor as a parent. Withstand! If they kill me, I will die with the words, 'Jesus and my fatherland.'" The Communists, enraged, fell upon the child and beat him to death, with blood spattered over the walls of the cell. He died praising God. Our dear brother Florescu was never the same after seeing this.[2]

In the middle of suffering, in the middle of persecution, Jesus offers peace. Jesus offers courage—courage that the world cannot comprehend.

"Be courageous! I have conquered the world."

Pastor Kim

Jesus Freaks is another book that opened my eyes as a student to the atrocities suffered for the name of Christ. Here's one excerpt that has played over and over in my mind for years. It took place in North Korea in the 1950s.

> For years, Pastor Kim and 27 of his flock of Korean saints had lived in hand-dug tunnels beneath the earth. Then, as the Communists were building a road, they discovered the Christians living underground.
> The officials brought them out before a crowd of 30,000 in the village of Gok San for a public trial and execution.

They were told, "Deny Christ, or you will die." But they refused.

At this point the head Communist officer ordered four children from the group seized and had them prepared for hanging. With ropes tied around their small necks, the officer again commanded the parents to deny Christ.

Not one of the believers would deny their faith. They told the children, "We will soon see you in heaven." The children died quietly.

The officer then called for a steamroller to be brought in. He forced the Christians to lay on the ground in its path. As its engine revved, they were given one last chance to recant their faith in Jesus. Again they refused.

As the steamroller began to inch forward, the Christians began to sing a song they had often sung together. As their bones and bodies were crushed under the pressure of the massive rollers, their lips uttered the words: "More love to Thee, O Christ, more love to Thee. Thee alone I seek, more love to Thee. Let sorrow do its work, more love to Thee. Then shall my latest breath whisper Thy praise. This be the parting cry my heart shall raise; More love, O Christ, to Thee."[3]

This is what Jesus meant by,

"… in Me, you may have peace."

History has recorded that the last breath uttered by many saints of God in the face of their tormenters is simply a hymn of praise to their Creator—a home-coming song of praise to their Father—a song expressing the peace of God in the midst of suffering. This is a peace that a lost world cannot comprehend. This is a peace that is available only through the Giver of peace.

Jim Elliot

Through Gates of Splendor is the last book I'll mention. Perhaps more than any other, this book helped to shape a theology of missions for an entire generation that followed, including my own. Over 50 years ago, Jim Elliot, missionary to the Auca Indians of Equador, discovered what it meant to die for the cause of Christ. He, along with four other missionaries, was speared to death in his attempt to bring the Gospel to the unreached Auca tribe, known to the outside world as savages and headhunters. But the story doesn't end there. The grieving widows of all five of the men continued the work in Equador eventually seeing the entire village come to faith in Jesus Christ, including the men who had speared their husbands.

Through the accounts of Jim's journals made available by his widow, Elisabeth Elliot, we discover a normal man who struggled in his daily walk with Christ. But we also discover a man who had purposed in his heart to make his life available for God's use, no matter the cost. On October 28, 1949, Jim wrote in his journal what has become part of his legacy:

> He is no fool who gives what he cannot keep to gain what he cannot lose.[4]

I could continue endlessly listing the accounts of men and women who have experienced exactly what Jesus meant in these verses of John 16. They understood what Jesus said about being courageous and having peace in the midst of suffering. They understood that there is a cost involved in following Christ. In America we know very little about what it means to suffer for Christ—what it means for there to be a cost involved—how it feels to gather for a worship service and wonder if this is the day that armed men will raid your gathering and murder every man, woman, boy and girl.

Here's my challenge to you. Read Christian biographies—especially those of Christian martyrs. Find out for yourself the struggles of Christ-followers all around the world. Let their stories birth a desire in you to move beyond the comfortable Christianity that perhaps you have come to idealize—the pancake Christianity that is so easy to adopt in American culture. Let their stories take root in your heart as you seek the courage of Christ everyday in your own walk with Him.

Feeding Your Appetite

Knowing the high cost that many Christians pay for their faith around the world, how does this knowledge change, encourage or challenge the way you view your own faith?

How does the peace that Jesus gives differ from the world's idea of peace? Why is it difficult for the world to understand peace in the midst of suffering?

Check out www.prisoneralert.com for a current list of Christ-followers around the world who are imprisoned for their faith in Jesus. List some of them here and begin praying for them by name.

Recommended Reading:
Tortured for Christ by Richard Wurmbrand
Jesus Freaks by The Voice of the Martyrs and DC Talk
Through Gates of Splendor by Elisabeth Elliot

The Discovery: Beyond the Jesus of Flapjacks and Grilled Cheese

Prisoner of Hope by Jesse Miller
Dietrich Bonhoeffer: A Biography by Eberhard Bethge
Fox's Book of Martyrs by John Fox

Your Discovery

17

That They All Might Be Target Team Members
John 17

"Our relationship with our fellows and our relationship with God are so linked that we cannot disturb one without disturbing the other."
- Roy Hession

My wife loves Target more than any other store on earth. I think she believes that God lives there. My kids are starting to believe it too. Rainy lovingly calls it "the store with the red balls" referring to the precision-placed round concrete slabs which resemble giant clown noses that adorn the front entrance like the pillars of a Gothic cathedral and welcome every worshiping family to the religious experience that is Target.

The Discovery: Beyond the Jesus of Flapjacks and Grilled Cheese

A trip to Target is sort of a routine treat for Tasha and the kids. I usually can't go due to some sort of important business venture like organizing the highlighters on my desk—something as imperative as to require my presence there and absence from Target. Nonetheless, I always wish them a hearty "Godspeed" and send them on their way.

They've got their visits down to a science now. They go in, get what they came for, quickly cruise the *Dora the Explorer* aisle for Rainy (but only to look), the *Thomas The Tank Engine* aisle for Zeke and finish up with a speedy pit stop at the random music kiosk where Rainy repeatedly and quite severely mashes the buttons to choose several of her favorite musical selections. Once Tasha figures out how we'll afford to buy Target a new kiosk, the trio makes their way to the checkout where a Target team member dressed in red and khaki pleasantly greets them. And let's not forget that a quick stop at Starbucks (conveniently located by the exit where the wafting scent of fresh coffee grounds woos each shopper and proceeds to devour every bit of cash in his/her wallet like a black widow woos her male counterpart and then proceeds to devour the head of the poor, unsuspecting arachnid—okay, that might be a bit extreme!) is often essential to a proper conclusion to the whole experience.

I've always found it intriguing that Target employees are referred to as *team members* rather than employees. It's a title that the higher-ups at Target have discovered comes across in a much more appealing way. They are not simply employees; they are members of a team. It is a title that denotes unity, participation and excellence. It is a title that conveys a sense of worth and value as one member of a group working together with other members for the same purpose. In all the Target stores I've been in, it's been obvious to me that this team mentality makes a huge difference in the attitudes and the performance of each member. There is a sense of drive—a sense of desire—a sense of excellence—a sense that there is a greater purpose or goal to which all team members are working toward together.

The sad reality is, in most churches and among most Christ-followers, this sense of unity, family and mission has gotten lost somehow. Often there is more unity among Target team members than there is among the people of God—the ones created to live together in community for the purpose of pointing a lost world to Jesus Christ.

In John 17, we get an up close and personal look at the intimate relationship Jesus had with His Father—a revealing look into Jesus' intimate prayer time just before He was to go to the cross to die for the sins of the world. The central theme of His prayer? Unity. Unity among believers. Unity among believers so that an unbelieving world might believe in Jesus. That was Jesus' plan for reaching the world. That is *still* Jesus' plan for reaching the world. The church, the body of believers, the ones who have received the unmerited mercy and grace of God—they are the plan. We are the plan. And yet sadly some of the meanest, foulest, disunified, screwed-up bunch of individuals are people who claim to be Christ-followers. We claim to love Jesus, but we hate each other. James, the half-brother of Jesus, put it bluntly:

> "With it (our tongues) we bless our Lord and Father, and with it we curse men who are made in God's likeness" (James 3:9).

That's hard to hear, but it's the truth. Here's what Jesus prayed that we need so desperately:

> "May they all be *one*, as You, Father, are in Me and I am in You. May they also be one in Us, so the world may believe You sent Me." (John 17:21).

There are a couple of highlights about unity from this chapter that I want you to notice. The first is found here in this verse.

The Connection

As Christ-followers we are to be connected to one another in much the same way that Jesus is connected to the Father and the Holy Spirit. Now, I'm not going to go into a deep theological treatise on the doctrine of the trinity. That's another book for another author for another time. But simply put, the Bible teaches that there is one

God who exists in three persons—the Father, the Son and the Holy Spirit. No analogy really works to try to explain this type of relationship. They all break down somewhere along the way and usually end up in heresy (and I'd very much like to avoid that path). But Scripture teaches clearly that *Jesus* is God, the *Father* is God, and the *Holy Spirit* is God, yet God is *one* God (i.e. 1 Thess. 1:3-5, 2 Cor. 13:13[1], Jn. 14:9, Matt. 28:19, Eph. 1:12-14, Deut. 6:4, etc.).

This connection that we all have as believers in Jesus should resemble the relationship that God, Jesus, and the Holy Spirit have with each other. This is perfect unity. Paul illustrated this connection beautifully:

> "For as the body is one and has *many parts*, and all the parts of that body, though many, are *one body*—so also is Christ ... Now you are the body of Christ, and individual members of it" (1 Cor. 12:12, 27).

This is the beauty of the body of Christ. There is diversity among its members, but there is unity as well. Not all of us can preach. Not all of us can sing. Not all of us can teach. But we can all serve in the individual capacities for which God has created us and designed us. That's why no job is too small. No body part is insignificant.

Can you imagine a friend coming to you and saying, "Dude, I just had the greatest idea! I'm going to cut off my left thumb because it totally annoys me. It gets in the way when I'm trying to eat lunch, and I always end up gnawing into it, mistaking my own blood for ketchup. I think I'd be better off without it. I've got another one anyway!" You would immediately rush your friend to the mental health hospital breaking every possible traffic violation in the process.

No part of the body is too small or too insignificant. If I lost my left thumb I'd never be able to play the guitar again. The same is true for the body of Christ. No part is less important than another. That was Paul's point in 1 Corinthians 12. And that's the connectedness that we all have as the body of Christ. We are individual members, intimately connected to one another, striving for the same goal—the same purpose—that an unbelieving world might come to know Jesus Christ. Now here's the second highlight about unity.

The Completion

Verse twenty-three says this:

"I am in them and You are in Me. May they be made *completely* one, so the world may know You have sent Me ..."

The word *completely* in the original language stems from the same word that Jesus shouted from the cross when He said, "It is finished!" It communicates the idea of finality and perfection. It's as if Jesus is praying, "Father, unify them so much that people on the outside looking in might see them functioning perfectly and completely as a team." The church in America is a long way from that now. We split and divide at the drop of a hat. We get our feelings hurt, so we hop around to another church or another small group. Or worse, we just give up on church altogether. This is probably where it hits home with our generation the most, so I want to say a quick word to all the church dropouts.

In the 60s and 70s, the church failed on many fronts to keep up with the shifting culture. As a result, the Volkswagen-driving hippies who were saved out of the Jesus Movement were forced to find community elsewhere. As a result, groups like Campus Crusade for Christ and Young Life developed out of a sense of urgency for a new generation trying to live for Christ but finding little acceptance within the four walls of the traditional church. And I can't blame them. The impact of these Christian groups is beyond calculation. Lives have been changed all over the globe because of them. In fact, I probably wouldn't be a follower of Christ today without the influence of my dad. And it was at a college ministry *outside* of a local church where he heard the Gospel and was saved.

But here's what I want to say. Christian groups and clubs *cannot* replace the local body of Christ. They cannot replace the local community of believers covenanting together on a regular basis and participating together in worship, service, evangelism, preaching, teaching, prayer, baptism, the Lord's Supper, accountability and the list goes on. There is simply no replacement for the local faith community. If you have found yourself in the church dropout category for whatever reason, find a church that is doing church like the New Testament commands and plug in there. Bottom line? Get in community.

I love the word *community*. Because that's exactly what we are and it's what we do. We are a comm—unity. And you cannot have community without *unity*. Unity doesn't mean that we all conform to some type of outward pattern where we look like we just stepped off the set of the Brady Bunch. We already saw what Paul said about unity. To be completely unified means that we are striving to love each other as Christ loves us. Guys, it means that we refuse to look at our sisters in Christ in lustful ways. Girls, it means that you are aware of the struggle with purity that we guys have and as a result you're careful about what you wear. It means that we are not jealous over who is dating who. It means that we are avoiding gossip and slander at all costs. And it means that Target team members should not be outdoing us when it comes to unity.

A former boss of mine once commented to me, "I used to go to church until I starting seeing those same people in the bars with me!" Ouch! The world is desperate for something genuine. And it's time for the church of God to rise up in a unified collective effort to love each other and love the world to Christ.

Feeding Your Appetite

Given the current state of the church in America in general, are the conditions right for the world to see Christ in and through us? Why or why not?

What function has the Lord given you in the body of Christ? What are some of the gifts that you feel like the Lord has given you as an individual member of the body of Christ? If you can't pinpoint at least one gift, study Romans 12:4-8 and 1 Corinthians 12:4-11 and ask the Holy Spirit to begin to show you how He has gifted you.

Do you have any unresolved conflict with or harbored bitterness toward another follower of Christ that you need to make right? If so, study Matthew 5:21-26 and come up with some actions steps to make that right.

If you are not connected and plugged in to a local church, challenge yourself to make that happen within the next month.

Your Discovery

18

The Look
John 18

"We are he-man woman haters
We feed girls to alligators
Our clubhouse burned down mighty low
But we've got a plan to make some dough!"
- The Little Rascals

Have you seen *the look*? You know *the look*. *The look* that says, "I'm hiding something!" I'm starting to see it on the faces of my kids. As they get older, *the look* shows up more frequently. *The look* shows up hiding in a closet complete with watery eyes and a bulge in the rear of the diaper. *The look* shows up immediately after a blood-curdling scream echoes through the house and gives away the position of the assailant. *The look* is often accompanied by gooey chocolate chips smattered and smeared over the face of the guilty party. *The look* is often holding something expensive and broken. *The look* is good at getting away quickly. *The look* is sneaky. *The look* is both adorable and deadly. *The look* will have you blowing putrid steam out of your head one minute and rolling on the floor holding your aching sides the next minute.

The look doesn't really change all that much as we progress through life. *The look* is still there but it's subtler. It's sneakier. It's the difference between a kamikaze warplane and a stealth fighter. But the effects are just as damaging. *The look* is especially prevalent within religious circles. *The look* is good about adopting the name *Christian* but underneath it's nothing like the real thing. *The look* is good at playing the part of a counterfeit. It's graceful. It's unassuming. And it's deadly.

John 18 begins the weekend of drama that tragically crescendoed with the crucifixion of Jesus. Thankfully the story doesn't end there. But for now, we'll focus on the events leading up to Christ's death—particularly His trial before Annas. In this conversation between Jesus and Annas, an assumption is made. Annas, the high priest of Jerusalem, made a prejudgment about Jesus—a judgment that assumed Jesus was hiding something—a judgment that assumed Jesus was a false teacher. A fake. A master of *the look*. A judgment that assumed the rise of another cult, another religious faction, another wolf in sheep's clothing. The problem was, Annas' assumption was totally wrong. The conversation picks up in verse nineteen:

> "The high priest *questioned Jesus* about His disciples and *about His teaching*. 'I have spoken openly to the world,' Jesus answered him. 'I have always taught in the synagogue and in the temple complex, where all the Jews congregate, and *I haven't spoken anything in secret*'" (John 18:19-20).

If you're still reading this far into the book, chances are you don't doubt that Jesus is who He said He was. You probably don't have the same assumptions that Annas had about Jesus. Nonetheless, Jesus' response gives us some good insight into the characteristics of truth. He told them that He always taught openly to the world and He never taught anything in secret.

The Truth Has No Secrets

For some reason, when I think of secret meetings, my mind immediately pulls up an image of the "He-Man Woman Haters Club" from *The Little Rascals*. You remember those, right? The secret meetings where Darla and the girls were not allowed—meetings that helped to shape the political landscape and economic drive of a poor working-class neighborhood—well, ... either that or meetings that helped the boys devise more clever ways to hate the girls.

Remember Froggie? He was, by far, my favorite character. When he spoke, something about his deep, raspy voice made everyone in the club stop and listen. I have a friend from college who sounds just like him, only his name is Freaky instead of Froggie. I've always been envious of him.

Now imagine the Little Rascals twenty years later as radical neo-Nazi skinheads. Secret meetings take on a new name. A new level. A new degree.

Jesus was well aware that if He ever held secret meetings, it would give the wrong appearance—the appearance that He was raising an insurrection against Rome. These types of religious fanatics were rampant throughout Jerusalem and Judea. They would gather a following just long enough to advance a minor attack against Rome. And without so much as blinking an eye, the Roman authorities would eradicate the rebels. But this mentality was completely antithetical to Jesus' purpose on earth. He never had secret meetings to discuss the Jewish takeover of Rome, though this is what many of His followers desired. This is what they were looking for in a Messiah. But this wasn't Jesus. He always taught in the open. He wanted people to understand who He was—that He was the fulfillment of the Old Testament—that He was the coming Messiah the prophets spoke about. So He taught publicly. He preached publicly. He healed publicly. He had nothing to hide.

In a world where cults and false teachers rise up almost as quick as the Hollywood divorce rate, we must maintain a discerning spirit if we are going to holdfast to the truth of God's Word. In Paul's second letter to Timothy, he encouraged him to

"Hold on to the pattern of *sound teaching* that you have heard from me ..." (2 Timothy 1:13).

What sound teaching?
The essential beliefs of the Christian faith. The fact that Jesus was born of a virgin, was God wrapped in human flesh, lived a perfect life with no sin, was crucified for the sins of the world, was gloriously resurrected in bodily form and will one day return again to this earth to receive His people and establish His eternal reign. This is the sound teaching Paul was talking about.

But why did he have to remind Timothy of this? Why does he remind us of this? Because

"The time will come when they (those who claim to know Christ) will not tolerate sound doctrine, but according to their own desires, will accumulate teachers for themselves because they have *an itch to hear something new*" (2 Timothy 4:3).

This is where we find ourselves in the 21st century. We want to hear something new. We want a new savior. The Jesus of the Bible is too generic. We want something that puts an itch in our ears. We want something fanciful. Something different. Something magical.

Fifteen years ago, David Koresh came on the scene claiming to be the Messiah. His delusion came to a tragic end when, after a 51-day standoff with federal agents, his Waco, Texas compound was burned to the ground. 80 bodies were pulled from the remains.[1] More recently, a self-proclaimed Hispanic Jesus has caught the attention of the world. This self-proclaimed messiah surrounds himself with beautiful women, covers himself in tattoos of the number *666*, drinks, smokes and pads his pockets. *The look* is everywhere.

Hopefully, you and I are too smart to follow a blonde-haired, blue-eyed, delusional American claiming to be Jesus. The problem is, most of Satan's deceptions do not come barreling down our *cul-de-sac* blowing the horn. Sometimes that works. But most often, the enemy is subtle. *The look* is hidden. That's why, as followers of Christ, we have to guard so carefully against false teaching. It shows up everywhere. It shows up in our pulpits. It shows up on Christian television. It's dressed nicely. It's packaged in a way that *resembles* the truth found in the Bible, but is the furthest thing from it.

Spotting the Imitation

I have a Taylor 410-CE acoustic guitar. Maybe that means nothing to you. I love this guitar. I've had it for ten years now. I saved up for it for several years as a high school student. I know this guitar. I know how it sounds. I am intimately familiar with its warm, deep tone. I know how it feels. I am innately accustomed to the feel of the ebony fret board and the Sitka spruce and ovangkol wood that make up the body. If you blindfolded me and put another guitar in my hands, even another Taylor, I would immediately know it. Why? Because I know my Taylor. I know the real thing. I'm so closely tied to my guitar, that I can immediately spot an imitation. Because an imitation that closely resembles the real thing is *still* an imitation.

Imitation Christianity is everywhere. It's rampant. You could make a full-time job out of watching and reporting on new ideas, new proposals and new religious systems that add to the Bible. You could devote all of your time and resources to the endless study of cults, factions and religious sects and still not have a grasp on them all. So I have a better idea. Know the real thing. Know the real Jesus. If you know the real Jesus, the flapjacks and grilled cheese are not that hard to spot.

Having said that, this will sound contradictory, but it's also true. As Christ-followers, we must be knowledgeable and mindful of the false teaching that surrounds us if we are going to be voices of truth in the face of error. A great resource that has helped me in discerning truth from error is a little formula that I got from Dr. Danny Akin, President of Southeastern Baptist Theological Seminary. He explained that discerning false teaching is as simple as doing the math. Here's what false teachers do:

(+) They add to the Bible by prophet, professor, or pen.
(-) They subtract from the person and work of Christ. They deny His eternal deity and find false or inadequate His atonement for salvation.
(x) They multiply the requirements for salvation if indeed they believe in salvation.
(✓) They divide our allegiance from God in Christ to others.[2]

Good stuff, Danny. Oops, gotta run. Zeke's hiding in the corner with *the look.*

Feeding Your Appetite

What imitation or counterfeit teachings have you heard recently that attacked the truth of the Gospel? Were they obvious or subtle?

Do you think the subtle imitations are deadlier than the obvious ones? Why or why not?

The Discovery: Beyond the Jesus of Flapjacks and Grilled Cheese

How does the fact that Jesus taught openly and publicly lend credibility to His message?

When you have some time, spend a few minutes on www.4truth.net and do some basic research on a couple of the major cults. List some of the ways they add to, subtract from, multiply, and divide the message of Christianity found in Scripture.

Recommended Reading:
The Case for Christ by Lee Strobel
Jesus Among Other Gods by Ravi Zacharias
Mere Christianity by C.S. Lewis
www.4truth.net

Your Discovery

19

More Dot Connecting
John 19

"It costs God nothing, so far as we know, to create nice things: but to convert rebellious wills cost Him crucifixion."
- C.S. Lewis

The Passion of the Christ spent a large portion of the film focused on this event. John only wrote one verse. I'm talking about the actual flogging of Jesus prior to His crucifixion. It was perhaps even more gruesome than the film depicts. Some scholars, doctors and historians believe that Jesus' intestines were likely protruding from the large open gashes in His flesh. It was a grueling form of torture, meant to bring the individual to the brink of death, but no further. The Romans perfected it.

In contrast to the movie, John's attention was directed more toward the crucifixion itself. However, he was less interested in the gory details than he was in communicating the original intention of his book—to record details that magnified and illustrated Jesus as the Messiah, the fulfillment of prophecy. As we'll see, John's consistent Messianic theme throughout the book also drives chapter nineteen. That's why, when we come to John 19, the crucifixion chapter, we discover numerous references to the Old Testament—references that were strategically placed throughout the crucifixion account—references that connect the dots of the crucifixion events with their partner prophecies. There are at least four clear references to Old Testament prophecy that this chapter highlights.

1. The Clothes – Connects to Psalm 22:18

> "So they said to one another, 'Let's not tear it, but toss for it, to see who gets it.' They did this *to fulfill the Scripture* that says: *They divided My clothes among themselves, and they cast lots for My clothing.* And this is what the soldiers did (John 19:24)."

Rather than discarding Jesus' clothes, the soldiers gambled for them. In a final act of humiliation, as Jesus' naked, bleeding, suspended body hung on the cross overtop of them, the soldiers rolled the dice for His clothes.

I wonder if the soldiers had any clue that as they played their little game, they were helping to solidify the Messianic title of the One they were killing—playing into the hand of God's providential workings in those final moments of Jesus' life. As they gambled for His clothes, they simultaneously helped to fulfill the Scriptures attesting to Jesus' authenticity.

And then I can't help but wonder how often you and I are guilty of similar games—"Christian" games that we play at the foot of Jesus' cross that blind us to who He really is. Games that distract us from the horror that's taking place just above us.

This Christmas, my brothers and I received a Nintendo Wii from my mom—a gift that we didn't know we wanted until she explained how she had waited for countless hours in sub-zero temperatures to obtain one of only fifty available. She forced a smile—one of those motherly, hairy eyeball, you-better-like-this types of smiles—

and then lovingly revealed to us the desire we had for the machine, though again, we were only just realizing that desire. We didn't argue. To show our appreciation, we played the time-wasting, full body-utilizing contraption around the clock.

To say that it was a distraction would be a severe understatement. An absolute diversion from all moral, social, and familial responsibility is more like it. In the moments that I found myself enveloped within the Wii's mind-altering web, all connection to reality was lost. Dad-duties were out the window. My kids seized the opportunity the Wii afforded them. Cats were in the microwave. Cousins were being tortured with ribbon and Lincoln Logs. Sharp objects found their wings. Large, mammoth objects found haven in the toilet tank. Neighbors reported blood-curdling screams to the authorities. You name it. It happened. I was distracted. I was mentally gone. The Wii had me in its grip and there was no turning back. The game I played was a game of distraction—a distraction from the reality happening all around me.

I often find myself in the shoes of the soldiers—playing games with little notice of Jesus' suffering. I forget He's there. I punch my list instead. Bible reading? Check. Prayer time? Check. Church attendance? Check. Fake smiles to fool the best? Check. Superficiality? Check.

The sad part about "Christian" distractions is that they make pitiful substitutions. They replace genuine devotion for temporary distraction. They replace love for Jesus with love for what *appears* to be Jesus—a love for pancakes.

2. The Wine – Connects to Psalm 22:15

"After this, when Jesus knew that everything was now accomplished *that the Scripture might be fulfilled*, He said, 'I'm thirsty'" (John 19:28).

I love the phrase, "when Jesus knew that everything was now accomplished." It captures the deity of Christ in the midst of the chaos. John 18:4 makes a similar statement prior to Jesus' arrest—both verses deliberately placed by the author to show that Jesus was in complete control of the situation—that none of the events of Jesus' trial or His death were merely circumstantial. God orchestrated them. His thirst on the cross? Purposeful. Intentional. Messianic. The sour wine became the precursor to His finished work on the cross.

And yet, even for those of us who claim to believe that Jesus knows everything and is in control of everything, the circumstances of life can lead us to believe otherwise. We are plagued by doubt. We doubt Him in the routine stuff of life. We doubt whether He will provide enough this month to pay our rent. We struggle to see why He lets us go through times of loss, death and sorrow. We wonder if He sees our hurt—if He knows our insecurities—if He really cares what we do with our lives. Surely John felt this. Standing at the cross watching all of this unfold, he probably doubted. He was probably scared to death. But years later, as he reflected back, he could say with 100% certainty, "Jesus knows all. Jesus sees all. Jesus fulfilled all. Jesus is all I need."

3. The Bones – Connects to Psalm 34:20

> "But one of the soldiers pierced His side with a spear, and at once blood and water came out ... For these things happened so *that the Scripture would be fulfilled: Not one of His bones will be broken*" (John 19:34, 36).

Physicians and scientists tell us that the actual cause of death by crucifixion is asphyxiation, or suffocation. In order to inhale, the victim would have to endure the excruciating pain of pushing up his weight with his feet. Once elevated, a breath was taken and the body would collapse once again, hands and arms tearing under the weight. On and on this would go, all for one breath. In order to speed up the process, the soldiers would break the legs of the person so that coming up for air was impossible. Suffocation would quickly follow.

Now, what's amazing about Jesus' death is that He didn't need the assistance of the soldiers. He died with all of His bones intact. And thus He fulfilled yet another prophecy—a prophecy that had little chance of coming to pass had Jesus not been who He claimed to be. Coincidence? Nope. God's ordered plan.

4. The Piercing – Connects to Zechariah 12:10

"Also, another *Scripture says*: *They will look at the One they pierced*" (John 19:37).

My kids have a baby Bible that someone gave them a few years ago. Its insanely bright blue cover foretells of the magic inside — more of the eye-blinding superfluity of color accompanied by bubbly, Little People-looking, Charlie Brown-resembling cartoon characters. Eye candy for the kids. Senseless cornea burning for Tasha and me. It's filled with key Bible stories that we often read to our kids before bedtime. The story about Jesus' death is one we read quite frequently. Wait! Just kidding. Actually we don't, because … IT'S NOT IN THERE! Unbelievably, Jesus' death is *absent* from the heretical fireworks show disguised as a baby Bible! Like you do with your weird second cousin at a family reunion, it's totally ignored. It skips one of the most crucial elements of the Christian faith — the fact that Jesus died a literal death on the cross. Maybe the author thought it was too grotesque for children. Maybe he thought neon colors and bubbly cartoon characters should be reserved for mangers, shepherds and angels rather than crosses, spikes and whips. I'm not sure. But one thing is certain; *my* children will know the truth.

John made it very clear that when Jesus was on the cross, He *literally* died. He *physically* died. He didn't just pass out or faint like your college professors might tell you. He died. The soldier who pierced Jesus' side was a professional executioner. When he speared Jesus, he thrust upward into the heart to ensure His death. And without His death, there can be no resurrection. Without His resurrection, our faith is worthless and we are still lost in our sins (1 Corinthians 15:17). The blood and water that flowed from Jesus' side was just another indicator of His literal death — an indicator that John emphasized to his readers as an actual eyewitness of this horrible event.

For me, the dots are connected. For many, the dots remain only dots. Scripture explains why.

"For to those who are perishing the message of the cross is *foolishness*, but to us who are being saved it is God's power" (1 Corinthians 1:18).

We can't always silence the opposition, because for them, this message is foolishness. But we *can* make sure that Jesus' death is forever the cornerstone that we build our lives upon. We *can* make sure that we never cease to share the only message that can save — the only message that can melt a hardened heart. We *can* make sure that we stay focused on Jesus and refuse the distractions. We *can* make sure that we rest in the fact that God is always in control no matter how out-of-control life may get.

Feeding Your Appetite

Are there currently any "Christian" games in your life that are distracting you from a genuine relationship with Christ? If so, what are some ways you can refocus on what really matters?

What are some typical doubts and insecurities that you face? How can you remain focused on the fact that God is always in control no matter how out-of-control the world might seem?

Take some time to thank Jesus for dying on the cross for your sins. Allow the reality of what He went through for you to soak in.

Take some time to study the Old Testament references that point to Jesus' suffering and crucifixion (Psalm 22:15, 18; 34:20; Zechariah 12:10). Ask the Holy Spirit to help you connect all the dots if there are any that remain unconnected.

Your Discovery

20

Do We Have Enough Canned Meat?
John 20

"Being really cold. I have been unfortunate enough to spend much of my life being really cold, and I lie at home now in a hot bath and complain to my wife that there's not enough hot water. She says, 'If people could know how pathetic you really are.'"
- Bear Grylls, answering the question, "Which is worse, being really hot or really cold?"

"**D**AD, WE'RE LOST," I interjected as the familiar surroundings of our rural farmhouse property dwindled behind us. Our adventure began only about ten minutes earlier. But due to my racing heart, clammy palms and constant wiping of my glistening brow, minutes seemed more like hours. My dad was our pack leader. Our troop consisted of Smooth and me. Our mission? To explore the vast expanse of wooded land that bordered the back of our property—probably no more than a half-acre, at best. But for nine-year-old boys it felt like a dense jungle with never-ending opportunities for lostness.

I couldn't help it. From deep within the caverns of my mind, movie clips came to life. I immediately thought of the Fire Swamp from *The Princess Bride* and imagined rodents of unusual size bounding like mutant, rabid squirrels from behind trees attaching their razor-sharp teeth into my neck and severing my jugular. I assured myself that if this happened, death would come quickly and painlessly—perhaps even as painless as the flesh wounds of severed limbs inflicted by King Arthur upon the Black Knight in *Monty Python and the Holy Grail*. Regardless, my feeling of being lost intensified as we moved deeper into the wood. Finally, a clearing appeared—a gravel road of sorts.

"Here we are," Dad exclaimed.

"This doesn't look familiar," Smooth said, his tone adding to my disconcertedness regardless of dad's air of confidence.

"WE'RE STILL LOST," I reminded everyone, as if their bleeding ears hadn't clued me in to the fact that they heard my blood-curdling epiphany the *first* time.

"No we're not, guys. We'll just draw a map here in the gravel and find our way home," Dad declared.

Okay. It's time to pause and brace for an earth-shattering revelation. Every red-blooded human being with as much as a parasite for a brain understands that unless you have a map to begin with, creating one in the middle of your lost condition offers exactly *zero* help. This was a concept completely foreign to Smooth and me. We thought it was a brilliant idea. *Draw a map! Perfect!* Dad was surely the smartest man on the planet. He made Bear Grylls' adventures on *Man vs. Wild* look like an episode of *Dora the Explorer*. Dad was a true wilderness man, or so we thought.

Within a couple of minutes Dad had sketched the most detailed map ever created using gravel, sticks and rock sediment. We studied the map, identified our route home and within a few minutes we were back in familiar territory. A stroke of genius—that or the fact that Dad was never lost to begin with. The latter was, of course, the reality though my mind would only allow me to believe that he was more cunning than Yogi Bear, Bear Grylls and Smokey the Bear all wrapped into one (and any other adventurer who had a knack for surviving in the great outdoors and who consequently happened to have *Bear* attached to his name). The truth was, Bear Dad knew where he was all along. He was never lost—that or the fact that he actually *was* lost and somehow by drawing shapes in the dirt he magically manipulated the corresponding landscape. But it's a safe bet that he simply knew where he was.

The fear that had paralyzed me and brought me within moments of soiling myself was induced by my limited perspective. The outcome that was so clear to Dad was foggy in my nine-year-old mind. It was senseless worry. Needless fear. Dad was always in control.

Perspective and Fear

Limited perspective is arguably one of the chief causes of fear. It paralyzes hope because of its narrow scope. It stifles courage because of its obsession with the here and now. Limited perspective short-circuits the power, strength and courage of God in our lives—a phenomenon with which the disciples were well acquainted during the two days of uncertainty and limbo between Jesus' death and resurrection. John explained the disciples' sentiment:

> "For *they still did not understand* the Scripture that He must rise from the dead" (John 20:9).

After three-and-a-half years of walking with Jesus, hearing His claims, observing His power and attesting to His deity, the disciples still did not understand that He must rise from the dead. They had heard all the right information, but it had gone in one ear and out the other. So it should come as no surprise when we discover the disciples completely shut in together, doors locked and boarded, ready for Hurricane Katrina. John explained:

> "In the evening of that first day of the week, the disciples were gathered together with *the doors locked* because of their fear of the Jews" (John 20:19).

Their focus had become the here and now. Their perspective was limited. Never mind the fact that Jesus had explained multiple times that this would happen. Never mind the fact that they had seen dead men rise. Never mind the fact that the disciples always saw a consistency in what Jesus claimed and in what they observed. Yet, none of this made any difference in the fallout shelter. Their focus was limited. They couldn't see past their own reality. All they knew was that this Jesus whom they followed for three-and-a-half years was now dead—really dead. After all, John had observed the whole ordeal at the foot of the cross. And now that Jesus was gone, fear surfaced—fear of the Jews—the guys that Jesus constantly ticked off. What hope could be found in such tragedy? What courage could be found in the face of such fear? What would it take to bring the disciples to their senses?

The disciples needed a change of perspective. They needed something to believe in. They needed the manifest presence of Jesus to eradicate their fear. And that's what they got.

From Fear to Boldness in 3.5 Seconds

"Then Jesus came, stood among them, and said to them, 'Peace to you!' Having said this, He showed them His hands and His side. So the disciples rejoiced when they saw the Lord" (John 20:19b-20).

I love that phrase, "Then Jesus came." His coming changed everything. Through one little turn of events, the disciples were radically transformed from a cowardly, cuddled-in-a-tub bunch of spring pansies, to a dynamic, fearless force that awakened the known world to the power of the life-changing message of Jesus. These eleven men became fearless mouthpieces for the Gospel and carried the message of the cross from continent to continent. They were now witnesses to the resurrection—the seventh sign—the culmination of Jesus' work on earth—and their fear was at once eliminated.

The fear that had once paralyzed them was now driven out by His very presence. Don't believe me? Look what happened a few months later in the book of Acts. Peter and John endured imprisonment and a ruthless beating for preaching the message of Jesus. Following the brutal attack, the men were threatened to speak no longer in the name of Jesus. Their backbone became obvious as they responded,

> "Whether it's right in the sight of God for us to listen to you rather than to God, you decide; for *we are unable to stop speaking* about what we have seen and heard" (Acts 4:19b-20).

No longer do we find Jesus' disciples boarded up in a dark room stocked with batteries, Spam and bottled water. The risen Christ dispelled the fear that had once consumed them. The risen Christ radically changed their perspective. And their actions that followed are perhaps the greatest argument for the resurrection of Christ.

The Big Question

Let's change gears for a minute. There are at least two audiences reading this. The first group believes the claims of Jesus and that He *was* actually, physically resurrected. The second group is not sure about the resurrection. The second group may think it's absolute nonsense. Or at very least, a myth. Regardless, both groups need to hear this.

There is one question that every resurrection-doubter must face. There's one question that none of us can get past.

Apart from seeing the risen Christ, what would cause Jesus' scared, freaked-out disciples to be transformed from fearful babies to bold warriors?

Answer? Nothing apart from attesting to and experiencing the risen Jesus could have infused the disciples with this type of boldness. Not just any type of boldness. Boldness in the face of death. The type of boldness that gives incredible evidence for the resurrection of Jesus.

But someone might say, "That's ridiculous! It was a conspiracy! Jesus never rose from the dead. Here's what happened. The disciples got together and determined to spread the lie that Jesus had risen from the dead in order to maintain what dignity they had left."

Good try, but there's a fatal flaw in this theory. Would you die for a lie? Maybe—if you didn't know it was a lie. But would you die for a lie that you *knew* definitively to be a lie? If you're honest and if I'm honest, the answer is *NO*! But history tells us that each one of the disciples endured incredible, inhumane deaths as they took the message of Jesus all over the world.

Here are some quick snapshots. James, the brother of John, was beheaded by order of Herod Agrippa. Philip was imprisoned in Heliopolis, tortured with whips and crucified. Matthew was cut to pieces with an axe in the city of Nadabah. James, the half-brother of Jesus, was stoned to death and his brains were bashed out with a large club. Andrew took the Gospel to many Asian countries and was eventually crucified. Peter was crucified upside down upon his own request. Bartholomew preached in several countries, translated the Gospel of Matthew into an Indian language and was eventually crucified. Simon traveled to Africa and Britain preaching the Gospel. He was crucified in Britain. John, the writer of John's Gospel, preached all over Asia. He was ordered to Rome where he was placed in a boiling cauldron of oil. Miraculously he survived and was banished to the Island of Patmos.[1]

And what about Thomas—the one who was missing when Jesus first appeared to the disciples? The one known as the doubter. What happened to him?

Thomas was chosen to go the remote tribes of North Africa where he witnessed many of the savage tribes come to faith in Jesus. He later traveled to Calamina, India where his faith was severely challenged. One day while observing the priests worshiping the image of the sun god, Thomas boldly destroyed the image causing immediate upheaval among the people. Dragging him before the king, the priests insisted that Thomas be thrown into a furnace of blazing fire. The order was given and Thomas was thrown in. Miraculously, however, he remained unharmed. The priests, now livid, speared him through with javelin-like fire pokers. His life? Extinguished. His faith? Strong to the very end.[2]

The Discovery: Beyond the Jesus of Flapjacks and Grilled Cheese

Their perspective had changed. They had seen the risen Christ. Cowering in a corner, the disciples experienced the actual presence of Jesus, and it changed the way they perceived everything. Everything that Jesus had taught them now came into crystal clear focus. And now they were willing to die for Him. More than that, they were willing to *live* for Him. They were willing to live every moment of the rest of their lives for Him as they took the Gospel to the farthest reaches of the planet. The fear that had once limited their perspective and led to a mistrust of all that Jesus had claimed, was at once dispelled by His presence.

As a boy, I followed my dad on numerous adventures. None that were actually dangerous, but I had watched enough movies to magnify what little danger that did exist into full-blown fear. Fear that was needless and pointless. Fear induced by my limited perspective. Always my biggest enemy. Always my biggest challenge. But on each and every adventure, Dad always came through. He always led me home. He always dispelled fear by his presence.

So, why should we continue to allow our limited perspective to paralyze us into fearful living? Why do we live as if the presence of Jesus is beyond our reach, reserved for the Billy Grahams of the world? Why are we content to live this way? If the risen Christ has appeared to you, if the Holy Spirit has taken up residence in your heart, don't continue to live in fear as if He hasn't. His presence is real. His presence can and should be experienced everyday of our lives. He is faithful. He never disappoints. He always comes through. He's alive and well. He is the risen Savior. Allow the permeating presence of Jesus to dispel the fear that so easily discourages, sets back and paralyzes.

"There is no fear in love; instead, perfect love drives out fear, because fear involves punishment" (1 John 4:18).

Feeding Your Appetite

How has your limited perspective incited fear in your life? How has it caused you to mistrust God?

Are there any fears in your life that are paralyzing you from being outspoken and bold for your faith in Christ? Ask the Lord to reveal His presence to you and ignite in you a boldness to proclaim the life-changing message of Christ to the people in your sphere of influence.

What other claims or arguments have you heard *against* the resurrection of Jesus? What are some ways you can better prepare yourself to answer skeptics?

Pray that the Holy Spirit will make you ever-aware of His presence in your life. And ask Him to help you live as if you believe it to be true.

The Discovery: Beyond the Jesus of Flapjacks and Grilled Cheese

Your Discovery

21

The Danish Red Fox and the Farmer: A Parable About Sin and Restoration
John 21

"... these are the times of dreamy quietude, when beholding the tranquil beauty and brilliancy of the ocean's skin, one forgets the tiger heart that pants beneath it, and would not willingly remember, that this velvet paw but conceals a remorseless fang."
- Herman Melville, *Moby Dick*

Suppose you are a brightly colored red fox living in the meadows of Denmark. And you have seemingly endless acres of wide-open fields and meadows in which to prance and frolic and enjoy the gaieties (as in *happy things*) of life that every deserving red fox should. Imagine that in this Danish meadow beautifully arrayed with luscious trees and shrubberies of various sorts, there is also a fence—a fence that acts as a barrier between you and the adjacent meadow to which it borders—a tall, barbed wire fence that you know would cause unnecessary and unwanted pain should you ever try to jump it.

Now, imagine that one day your curiosity gets the best of you. The closer you get to the fence, the more you convince yourself that you can jump over it and enter the additional endless Danish meadows that await your exploration and fox-like gaiety (as in *happiness*). You debate with yourself.

"Should I jump? Should I not? After all, I am a red fox. And I'm Danish. And Danish red foxes are meant to frolic in open meadows. And Danish red foxes can jump high. So, since I'm a high-jumping, meadow-deserving, frolicking gay (as in *happy*) *Danish red fox, I think I'll jump."*

You make up your mind to take the leap. You decide that backing up to gain additional runway is a good idea. You do that. Now you're ready.

You take off with speed never before experienced by any Danish red fox, especially frolicking gay ones (as in *happy ones*). You take flight. As you begin your ascent, a fox-shattering thought occurs to you. HORROR OF HORRORS! You may have underestimated the height of the fence. Your front legs clear the razor-sharp barbs. Whew! But as you make your descent down the other side, your back legs snag the wire.

"HEAVENS!" you scream, as your hind legs become entangled in the cursed wire ripping and tearing as the barbs grab and lock into place in your tender Danish red fox flesh. You hang suspended. Tearing. Pulling. You're stuck. You're in tremendous pain—pain never before experienced by any other gay (as in *happy*) Danish red fox. You're losing blood. Your vision is blurry. Wait! What's that sound?

To be continued …

Sin and Failure

Peter. The man who said he would rather die than to deny Jesus. The man who cut off the right ear of Malchus, servant of the high priest, trying to defend Jesus from the mindless mob who came to arrest Him. The man who had once made a declaration that he would never desert Jesus saying,

> "Lord who will we go to? You have the words of eternal life" (6:68).

This is the man who was also known for sticking his foot in his mouth out of gut reaction to the moment. Never had he lodged his foot so deep down his oral cavity than on the night he denied Jesus three times. Remember the scene back in John 18? As Jesus was going on trial in front of Annas, Peter was following along at a distance trying to disguise himself among the crowd. As he was warming himself by the fire, he was asked on three separate occasions whether or not he was one of Jesus' disciples. Each time Peter denied any association with Jesus. Each time becoming more and more entangled in the barbed wire into which he jumped.

Days later on a fishing expedition, we still find Peter dangling from the fence, legs torn and bleeding from the sharp barbs in which he had entwined himself. It was a predicament of his own choosing. His own demise. And he needed help. No, he needed more than help. He needed forgiveness and restoration. He needed an audience with the Savior whom he had denied a few days earlier.

Jesus knew all this. He knew Peter's situation. He knew about Peter's failure. He knew about his denial. He knew Peter's feelings of unworthiness. He knew that Peter needed to be forgiven and restored. So, Jesus set the stage for the tough conversation. Jesus set the table for the breakfast conflict. Peter was about to have breakfast with Jesus—with the real Jesus—the Jesus who offers forgiveness from our failures—the Jesus who restores and makes new—who takes the dirty rags of a sin-infested life and transforms them into clothes fit for a king. But the process isn't easy. The process hurts.

The Farmer

... You're losing blood. Your vision is blurry. Wait! What's that sound? It sounds like footsteps. They're getting closer. Closer. A blurry, tall object, upside down from your condition, enters your field of vision.

"OH, MUSKRAT" you bellow, cursing the name of the one creature that you detest more than any other. "IT'S A DANISH MAN!" A farmer to be exact. The farmer who happens to own the beloved meadow in which you frolic and partake in merriment.

"Surely he has come to make a quick meal of me," you tell yourself as you writhe and wiggle all the more.

The farmer reaches out in your direction and begins to pull on the wire. OH, THE PAIN! He begins to tug and maneuver the barbs in order to free them from your flesh. And, oh, the searing pain! Oh, the throbbing of your wounds! The pain is excruciating!

"Why doesn't he finish me off quickly?" you wonder to yourself. But then, something odd happens. You discover that your hind legs are not so entangled anymore. Could it be?

"Is the farmer freeing me?" you ask yourself. *"Surely not. After all, I'm certainly nothing but a menace to him anyway."*

But you quickly discover that your hypothesis was correct. The beloved Danish farmer has freed you. He is now bandaging your wounds. He is dressing them. The pain is still there. The dressing hurts. The mending is uncomfortable. The pain. The healing. The pain. The mending. The pain. The restoration.

Pain and Healing

Peter needed mending. Peter needing healing. But the process was painful. The process was grueling.

"When they had eaten breakfast, Jesus asked Simon Peter, 'Simon, son of John, do you love Me more than these?' 'Yes, Lord,' he said to Him, 'You know that I love You.' 'Feed My lambs,' He told him. A second time He asked him, 'Simon, son of John, do you love Me?' 'Yes, Lord,' he said to Him, 'You know that I love You.' 'Shepherd My sheep,' He told him. He asked him the third time, 'Simon, son of John, do you love Me?' Peter was grieved that He asked him the third time, 'Do you love Me?' He said, 'Lord, You know everything! You know that I love You.' 'Feed My sheep,' Jesus said" (John 21:15-17).

Three times a denial. Three times a confession. Hardly equal by human measurement, but nonetheless equal in value. Jesus made the assessment. This is what Peter needed—the thing that hurt the most. And Jesus did it right there on the beach over breakfast in front of Peter's friends. Ouch. Why? Because these guys needed to see for themselves Jesus' revalidation of Peter. Jesus knew that Peter had to regain their trust. Jesus had plans of using Peter to build His Church. He had already made that clear (Matthew 16:18). These guys remembered that promise and knew that they were supposed to be a part of that. Now, Jesus needed not only to restore Peter, but also to revalidate his position in the eyes of these guys—the ones who would follow Peter to the death.

Restoration hurts. Healing hurts. It hurt Peter in a lot of ways.

A Tainted View of Restoration

And isn't that where we find ourselves so often? In that place of suspension, tangled up in the mess that we brought on ourselves? Already hurting from the pain we caused ourselves, and now Jesus wants to inflict more pain? Why, Jesus? Can't you restore me without more pain? You're the great healer. And on and on we go reacting like the fox. Kicking. Screaming. Pulling away from His hand of healing. We become less aware of the pain that we originally inflicted on ourselves and more focused on the pain God is causing by trying to bring healing. And so our view of restoration becomes tainted. Here's another story to illustrate this misconception.

I've already confessed to my propensity toward having brown thumb of the animalia kingdom. Another story here will relieve any doubts you may have had about that.

Tasha and I used to have a goldfish named Moby. I say "used to" because, as you might imagine where this story is headed, these are key words—bridge-building words, if you will. We named him Moby after his hero, Moby Dick, the whale. And though our Moby was no whale, he was at least a fish. And though we couldn't be certain that Moby Dick was indeed Moby's hero, since he could neither confirm nor deny such a fact, we went with our gut.

Being as we were newly married (that is, Tasha and I—not Moby and I) and very poor, we decided that a cleaning unit for Moby's tank was an unnecessary expenditure. Thus, I would do the honors of cleaning the tank whenever the green film of mucous and feces became too much of an eyesore. Such was the task to which I was committed on that fateful day—that, oh so, memorable day.

As was my routine, I scooped Moby out of his tank with a nylon net and placed him temporarily in a smaller holding cell. Then, after putting on my HASMAT gear, I began cleaning the tank in the kitchen sink using scalding hot water, Dawn dish detergent and a sponge.

Mind you, the tap water was running—always running. And scalding—always scalding. But it wasn't my fault. Someone should have told me not to place Moby's holding cell in the same sink where the hazardous materials were being detoxed. I don't know how the little feller managed to scoot his tiny residence under the direct flow of the scalding stream, but he did. As my mind wandered off somewhere within its hollow caverns and tunnels, and as my eyes became fixated upon random shiny objects, Moby's temporary tank began filling up. Finally snapping out of my daze, I quickly evaluated the situation and felt that pulling Moby out of the direct line of fire seemed like a good decision.

I did. But not before the boiling water had done its damage. Moby lay motionless, flipped on his side with a massive protruding belly. HORROR OF HORRORS! I had cooked his insides! I had boiled his bowels. I had incinerated his innards! I had fried my fish. I had mutilated my Moby! My only thought now was, *"How can I hide this from Tasha?"* But it was too late. She walked in the kitchen to see Moby floating on his side, waving one fin high in the air, as if preaching his own farewell discourse. I had goofed. I had made an ever-so-tiny error in my judgment. I had inflicted needless pain on my precious Moby, and it was completely my fault.

As you wipe the tears, let me draw the analogy for you. Whether we want to admit it or not, this is often our view of God. Rather than viewing Him as a loving farmer who is trying to untangle us from the wreckage, we view Him as One who inflicts unnecessary and undeserved pain on His children. Perhaps our view of Him is that of a bumbling, half-wit God doing the best He can, often sending needless pain our way. Or, on the other extreme, maybe God is more comparable to Sid from *Toy Story* who gets kicks and giggles out of watching us squirm in pain. Whether we put it in these terms or not, the fact is, we often pull away from His hand of healing and view it as senseless and undeserved.

Rather than acknowledging that it's our sin that has gotten us in this predicament to begin with, we curse and fuss and argue with God about the additional pain that it takes to bring about the necessary healing. We fight and fume and struggle against His hand of healing. That's why Peter responded the way he did. Verse seventeen says that Peter was *grieved* when Jesus asked the same question yet a third time. Peter fought it. It was painful. Maybe he thought it was easier just to give up—to take the easy way out.

Unbearable?

And isn't that the temptation for us? To give up? When the pain seems unbearable. When the task seems too difficult. When a friend dies without Christ and you never shared with him. Should you give up then? When you go weeks without a consistent time with God. Should you give up then? When you end up having sex with your girlfriend? Should you give up then? When you deny that you are a follower of Jesus. Should you give up then? When you think God can't forgive you. Should you give up then?

I have a friend who's enrolled in a Christian college—a girl who was once sold-out to Christ—totally in love with Jesus. The other day she confessed to Tasha that she's been contemplating giving it all up because it's too hard. "The Christian life is too tough," she said. And sometimes my flesh just wants to look people like that in the eye and say "boo hoo." Do you think it wasn't hard for Jesus? He endured the hellacious, sadistic torture of a Roman crucifixion so that you could go free. And it's "too tough" for you? Would it help if it was a little less difficult on you?

Oh, I've got it! We could just forget what's required of us and pretend this little verse doesn't exist.

"I assure you: A slave is not greater than his master ..." (John 13:16).

And rather than taking up our cross daily (Luke 9:23), maybe we could just follow behind at a safe distance holding our handkerchiefs instead, watching Jesus do all the work. Let's see how that works out for us!

Christ took on the sin of the whole world, including the sin to which you may be clinging right now—the sin of pride. The sin of thinking that it's all about you. That the Christian life should be a lovely bed of roses, clouds and care bears, and pot-luck suppers. The problem is, that's pseudo-Christianity. Pancake Christianity. Christianity that quits when it gets tough. Christianity that throws in the towel when you get pinned against the ropes.

So to you, friend, who is considering throwing in the towel and giving up on your Christian journey, I want to say this. Don't do it! Don't throw it all away. Is the Christian life hard? Absolutely! Is it filled with ups and downs? Most definitely! Does it hurt when we sin? Oh, yea. Does it hurt when Jesus takes us through that difficult process of healing and restoration? No question. But is the Christian life the most rewarding life to live? Is a life committed to Jesus Christ a life worth living? Without a doubt!

When the pain is excruciating, don't throw in the towel. Don't give up. Don't take the easy way out. Certainly, none of us are beyond committing the grossest of sins. Yet none of us are too far out of God's reach, either. I love what Jerry Bridges said about this.

> We should always view ourselves both in terms of what we are in Christ, that is, saints, and what we are in ourselves, namely, sinners.[1]

A Second Chance

Between John 18 and 20, Peter didn't have the right perspective. We don't know exactly his intentions for going back to fishing (his original occupation before Jesus called him three-and-a-half years earlier). He could have been well-intentioned. He could have been trying to provide for his family. We don't know. But the point is, he was really close to throwing it all away. He was walking the line. He screwed up and he probably contemplated walking away from it all.

But Jesus gave Peter a second chance. And John filled us in on the heart of Jesus by painting a portrait with specific and critical words that connect and link back to other events. Notice how the details link together:

1. Jesus originally called Peter out of fishing – Jesus taught Peter how to fish so He could call him again (21:6).
2. Jesus built a charcoal fire (21:9) – Peter denied Jesus by a charcoal fire (John 18:18).
3. Three denials (18:15-17, 25-27) – Three questions (v.15-17).
4. Jesus fed 5,000 men with fish and bread (John 6:1-14) – Jesus fed Peter with fish and bread (21:13), and in turn told Peter to "Feed my sheep" (21:17).

Absolutely none of these details are coincidental. They are all visual aids and literary devices that reinforce Jesus' restoration of Peter. They are all purposeful and intentional to drive home the truth that God is a God of second chances. I hope you grasp that truth as we wrap up this study.

The enemy wants nothing more than for you to finish this study discouraged and defeated. To become discouraged by failure. To believe that quitting while you're ahead is the best option. To believe the lie that God only uses perfect people. To believe that God's hand of healing should be avoided. To believe that God's hand of restoration causes senseless and needless pain. All of this is flapjack theology. The enemy knows it and wants you to believe it.

Peter is a living example—a living example of a broken, wounded life entangled in the barbed wire of his own poor decisions—yet, God took him and made something beautiful out of his life. He restored him. He healed him. And Peter became one of the greatest missionaries who ever lived. Through Peter's leadership, a wave of revival swept through 1st century Judaism, and God's Church was birthed—the Church that you and I are apart of!

Feeding Your Appetite

In what ways have you pulled away from God's hand of healing and restoration in your life?

Knowing that a strongly-committed follower of Christ like Peter can sin and then be restored, how does this give you encouragement in your own journey as you struggle to follow Christ?

As a follower of Christ, have you ever had thoughts of throwing in the towel and quitting? If so, what were the circumstances surrounding those thoughts? Consider for a moment how that could be a slap in the face to Jesus who paid such a high price for you.
Pray that God will give you His perspective on sin and restoration.

List some goals you have for moving ahead in your daily time with God and His Word, because having no plan is already a failed plan.

Your Discovery

CONCLUSION

Coming Back for Seconds

Among the many remarkable talents of which my wife is capable, there is one that takes the cake. She teaches our children sign language before they are able to speak. It's phenomenal! She read about it in a parenting book long before our kids were born. And it has made all the difference as far as our parental sanity is involved. It's a proven fact: When kids reach a certain age, they are capable of communicating with sign language. And usually this happens long before they can communicate with words. So Tasha teaches them the essentials—*hungry*, *thirsty*, *all done*, *more* and a few others. Signing alleviates a lot of the parental stress involved in trying to discern the difference between long grunts,

"I think Rainy is pooping her pants. No, ... wait, she's singing 'Jesus Loves Me.'"

low squeaks,

"I think Zeke wants another animal cracker. No, ... wait, he's actually suffocating on a care bear!"

quick yelps,

"Rainy must have pinched her finger in the lip of her sippy cup. No, ... wait, she's actually cheering for Elmo as he poops in the big-boy potty."

and harsh screams.

"Zeke must have tripped over his legos and busted his lip wide open again. No, ... wait, he's just screaming out the chorus of 'Letting Go of Tonight' by Underoath."

By now, you may be able to guess Zeke's favorite sign. *More*. *More* raisins. *More* milk. *More* pizza. *More* hamburger. *More* rolls. *More* French fries. You name it. *More* food. He always wants more. As soon as dinner is over, he dashes for the pantry.

That's been my whole desire for writing this book—to leave you wanting more. More of God. More of His Word. More of the Spirit's prevailing presence in your life. More of a hunger and desire to know God more intimately through Scripture, through prayer and through a personal relationship with the God of the universe.

You may not have all the right words to express to God your feelings and your desires. You may be new to this discovery. You may still be learning how to communicate with this indescribable God who created the shining stars in the heavens and the beating heart in your chest. But the beautiful thing is, God knows. He knows your heart. He knows your desires. He knows what you're trying to say even when you don't. Romans 8:26 says this:

> "In the same way the Spirit also joins to help in our weakness, because we do not know what to pray for as we should, but the Spirit Himself intercedes for us with unspoken groanings."

He knows your groanings. He knows when you truly want more of Him—when you want more of His Word—more of His power—more intimacy and closeness with Him. He knows. He understands. He can read your signs.

I hope that's where you've landed as this study concludes. I hope that you won't stop here. I hope that through this simple study of such a powerful book, you will be challenged to move ahead—to move forward in your understanding of the real Jesus of the Bible.

And as you know the real Jesus, you will begin to know yourself better.

So let me encourage you to have a plan. Set some goals in your personal relationship with Jesus.

Have a Bible reading plan. This is one of the best decisions I ever made. I try to read through the entire Bible every year. It sounds like a lot, but it only takes three chapters a day. I would encourage you to make that your goal from now until this time next year. But don't just read it to check it off your list. Read it intentionally. Let His Word soak into you—to change you—to reveal who He is—and who you are in Him. Also, check out www.deliberatepeople.com (a ministry started by Phil Joel, former bass player for the Newsboys) for free Bible reading plans and resources.

If reading the entire Bible is too intimidating at first, read through some of the smaller books to begin with. But read whole books at a time so you can begin to see how all of God's Word fits together as one big beautiful story of salvation.

Have a prayer plan. Commit to spending a certain amount of time talking to God every day. Make this time intentional. Get away from distractions. If you're anything like me, it might help you to actually journal your prayers to God. This is a great way not only to stay focused, but also to look back on to see how God answered your prayers.

Have a faith-sharing plan. As God begins to shape, mold and transform you from the inside out, be intentional about sharing with people about what God has done in your life. Don't be ashamed of it. Everyone has a story. And every story is unique. Let God use your story to reach into the lives of your friends, relatives and co-workers in a way that only your story can.

And every time you take a bite of a pancake or grilled cheese sandwich, let it be a reminder to you to always passionately pursue the real Jesus of the Bible. To love Him with all of your heart, soul, mind and strength.

The Discovery: Beyond the Jesus of Flapjacks and Grilled Cheese

Josh, Ezekiel, Areyna and Tasha Via

The grateful author would like to thank his family for their endless love and support throughout this project. Tasha was a particular help to Josh providing a constant flow of homemade white chocolate mochas and kisses (also homemade) throughout the writing process. He would also like to thank his friends, pastors and family involved in editing, critiquing and sharing in ideas, insights and graphic ideas.

Notes

Introduction: Breakfast with Jesus

1. Local6.com, "Couple claims Jesus appeared on pancake," http://www.local6.com/news/6880241/detail.html, Accessed January 8, 2008.
2. 9News.Com, "Woman cashes in on 'holy pancake,'" http://www.9news.com/news/watercooler/article.aspx?storyid=80955, Accessed December 13, 2007.
3. Buck Wolf, "Hungry for Miracles? Try Jesus on a Fish Stick," http://abcnews.go.com/Entertainment/WolfFiles/story?id=307227&page=1, Accessed December 13, 2007.
4. Richard Greenham, *Works,* 1612, p. 42. Quoted in Simon Chan, *Spiritual Theology* (Downers Grove, IL, InterVarsity Press, 1998), p. 158.

Chapter 1: Buzz Lightyear Recognition Software

1. Josh McDowell, *More Than a Carpenter* (Wheaton, IL: Living Books, Tyndale House, 1977), p. 107.
2. Ibid., p. 108.
3. William D. Mounce, *Basics of Biblical Greek* (Grand Rapids, MI: Zondervan, 1993), pp. 28-29.

Chapter 3: Novelty and Familiarity

1. John E. Reiley, www.texastavern-inc.com, Accessed September 5, 2007.
2. *Smooth* was a nickname that went back to the dawn of my brother's creation, or at least to the dawn of his teenage days when it was apparent to all that he was "smooth" with the ladies.
3. Publilius Syrus, *Maxim 640*.
4. Homer, *Iliad,* xxi., 379, 380. Quoted in Marvin R. Vincent, *Vincent's Word Studies in the New Testament* (Epiphany Software, 1999).
5. Ibid., xxi., 461, 467.
6. Stevie Wonder, "Heaven is 10 Zillion Light Years Away," *Fulfillingness' First Finale* (Motown Records, a Division of UMG Recordings, original recording 1974, 2000).

Chapter 4: Hey, Check Out That Random, Shiny Object!

1. Kenneth Gangel, "John," *The Holman New Testament Commentary, Vol. 4,* ed. Max Anders (Nashville, TN: Holman, 2000), p. 77.
2. Ibid.

Chapter 5: Storm Tracking with Crippled Guys

1. Kenneth Gangel, p. 77.

Chapter 6: To Whom Shall We Go?

1. Consequently, this is why the early church was accused of cannibalism. People outside of the church did not understand the metaphor and symbolism of the body and blood of Christ observed in communion.
2. Bill Nichols, *Usatoday.com,* March 07, 2006. Accessed September 17, 2007.
3. Marvin R. Vincent, *Vincent's Word Studies in the New Testament* (Epiphany Software, 1999).

4. Dietrich Bonhoeffer, *Discipleship,* quoted in *Dietrich Bonhoeffer Works, Vol, 4,* ed. Wayne Whitson Floyd, Jr., trans. Barbara Green and Reinhard Krauss (Minneapolis, MN: Fortress Press, 2003), p. 176.
5. Ibid.

Chapter 7: Identity Crisis – Part 1

1. Rich Mullins, "A Message to the Media," Creation Festival Radio Special, Mt. Union, PA, June 27, 1996; quoted in James Bryan Smith, *Rich Mullins: An Arrow Pointing to Heaven* (Nashville, TN: Broadman & Holman, 2000), p. 29.
2. Rich Mullins and Beaker, "Creed," BMG Songs, Inc. (ASCAP), Kid Brothers of St. Frank Publishing (ASCAP), 1993, *A Liturgy, a Legacy and a Ragamuffin Band* (Nashville, TN: Reunion, 1993).
3. Kenneth Gangel, pp. 152-153.
4. C.S. Lewis, *Mere Christianity and The Screwtape Letters: Complete in One Volume* (New York, NY: HarperCollins, 2003, *Mere Christianity* original copyright 1952), p. 52.

Chapter 8: Identity Crisis – Part 2

1. Louie Giglio, *I Am Not But I Know I AM* (Sisters, OR: Multnomah, 2005), p. 38.

Chapter 9: The Problem of Evil as it Relates to Chick-fil-A Cows

1. Peter Enns, "Exodus," *The NIV Application Commentary* (Grand Rapids, MI: Zondervan, 2000), p. 573.
2. Thomas Aquinas, *Summa Theologiae, 1a.13.3*
3. Laird R. Harris, Gleason L. Archer, Jr., and Bruce K. Waltke, *Theological Wordbook of the Old Testament* (Chicago, IL: Moody Press, 1980). Software Version.

Chapter 10: God Loves Dumb Animals

1. Another nickname from childhood also involving girls. You might be noticing a trend here!
2. Roy Hession, *The Calvary Road* (Fort Washington, PA: Christian Literature Crusade, 1950), p. 34.
3. Ibid.
4. Will Womble, an interview quoted in Johnny Hunt, *The Shepherd and His Sheep: One Day Leadership Conference* workbook.

Chapter 11: A Boy and Three Bears: A Parable About Faith and Doubt

1. Kenneth Gangel, p. 226.
2. Jerry Bridges, *The Discipline of Grace: God's Role and Our Role in the Pursuit of Holiness* (Colorado Springs, CO: Nav Press, 1994), p. 18.

Chapter 12: Where Feet and Hair Collide

1. Kenneth Gangel, p. 232.
2. Robert Jamieson, A. R. Fausset, and David Brown, *Commentary on the Whole Bible* (Grand Rapids, MI: Zondervan, 1961), p. 1444.

Chapter 13: Reinstate Slavery

1. http://www.rockonthenet.com/archive/1996/main.htm. Accessed December 6, 2007.
2. Eric Bazilian, "One of Us," performed by Joan Osborne, *Relish*, UMG Recording Inc., 1995.

Chapter 14: Directionally Challenged

1. Josh McDowell, pp. 111-112.
2. Ibid., p. 112.

3. Douglas Groothuis, *Truth Decay: Defending Christianity Against the Challenges of Postmodernism* (Downer's Grove, IL: InterVarsity Press, 2000), p. 11.
4. Joel Belz, *World*, July 12-19, 1997, p. 5; quoted in John Piper, *A Godward Life, Book 2* (Sisters, OR: Multnomah, 1999), p. 217.

Chapter 15: Obsessed with Foliage

1. Ernest Legouvé, quoted in Vern McLellan, *Wise Words and Quotes* (Carol Stream, IL: Tyndale House, 1998), p. 218.

Chapter 16: A Time is Coming

1. Richard Wurmbrand, *Tortured for Christ* (Bartlesville, OK: Living Sacrifice Book Company, 30th ed.), pp. 34-35.
2. Ibid., p. 34.
3. DC Talk and The Voice of the Martyrs, *Jesus Freaks: Stories of Those Who Stood for Jesus* (Tulsa: OK, Albury Publishing, 1999), pp. 124-125.
4. Elisabeth Elliot, ed., *The Journals of Jim Elliot* (Grand Rapids, MI: Fleming H. Revell, 1978), p. 174.

Chapter 17: That They All Might Be Target Team Members

1. In most translations, the reference for this verse is actually 2 Corinthians 13:14. The HCSB, which I am using throughout this book, is one verse short because it combines the traditional referencing of verses 12 and 13 into one verse.

Chapter 18: The Look

1. Timothy Miller, "Branch Davidians," *Microsoft Encarta Encyclopedia Standard 2004*.
2. Daniel Akin, "The gods of This Age and the Issue of Truth," a message delivered at SEBTS, Wake Forest, NC, World View Conference, February, 2006.

Chapter 20: Do We Have Enough Canned Meat?

1. John Fox, *Fox's Book of Martyrs,* Epiphany Software, 1999.
2. DC Talk and The Voice of the Martyrs, pp. 57-58.

Chapter 21: The Danish Red Fox and the Farmer: A Parable About Sin and Restoration

1. Jerry Bridges, p. 32.

Printed in the United States
127035LV00002B/1-144/P